D1195961

A THEOLOGY OF SOUTHEAST ASIA

A THEOLOGY OF SOUTHEAST ASIA

Liberation-Postcolonial Ethics in the Philippines

AGNES M. BRAZAL

ORBIS BOOKS
Maryknoll, New York 10545

Founded in 1970, Orbis Books endeavors to publish works that enlighten the mind, nourish the spirit, and challenge the conscience. The publishing arm of the Maryknoll Fathers and Brothers, Orbis seeks to explore the global dimensions of the Christian faith and mission, to invite dialogue with diverse cultures and religious traditions, and to serve the cause of reconciliation and peace. The books published reflect the views of their authors and do not represent the official position of the Maryknoll Society. To learn more about Maryknoll and Orbis Books, please visit our website at www.maryknollsociety.org.

Copyright © 2019 by Agnes M. Brazal

Published by Orbis Books, Box 302, Maryknoll, NY 10545-0302.

All rights reserved.

No part of this publication may be reproduced or transmitted in any form or by any means, electronic or mechanical, including photocopying, recording, or any information storage or retrieval system, without prior permission in writing from the publisher.

Queries regarding rights and permissions should be addressed to: Orbis Books, P.O. Box 302, Maryknoll, NY 10545-0302.

Manufactured in the United States of America.

Library of Congress Cataloging-in-Publication Data

Names: Brazal, Agnes M., author.
Title: A theology of Southeast Asia : liberation-postcolonial ethics in the Phillippines / Agnes M. Brazal.
Description: Maryknoll : Orbis Books, 2019. | Includes bibliographical references and index.
Identifiers: LCCN 2018037253 (print) | LCCN 2018047069 (ebook) | ISBN 9781608337583 (ebook) | ISBN 9781626982925 (pbk.)
Subjects: LCSH: Christian ethics—Catholic authors. | Christian ethics—Philippines. | Postcolonial theology—Philippines. | Liberation theology—Philippines.
Classification: LCC BJ1249 (ebook) | LCC BJ1249 .B623 2019 (print) | DDC 241.09599—dc23
LC record available at https://lccn.loc.gov/2018037253

Contents

Part II
Liberation-Postcolonial Ethics:
Contemporary Themes

Series Foreword

Duffy Lectures in Global Christianity

Catherine Cornille

Never, in the history of Christianity, has Christian faith been expressed in so many forms. Although long a global religion, it is only in the course of the twentieth century that the church came to valorize and celebrate the particularity of the different cultures and that local churches were creatively encouraged to engage and appropriate indigenous symbols, categories, and modes of celebration. A milestone in the Catholic Church was the 1975 apostolic exhortation *Evangelii Nuntiandi*, which states:

> The individual Churches, intimately built up not only of people but also of aspirations, of riches and limitations, of ways of praying, of loving, of looking at life and the world, which distinguish this or that human gathering, have the task of assimilating the essence of the Gospel message and of transposing it, without the slightest betrayal of its essential truth, into the language that these particular people understand, then of proclaiming it in this language. (no. 63)

The term *language* is here understood in the broad anthropological and cultural sense to touch on not only translation of the gospel message, but also "liturgical expression . . . catechesis, theological formulation, secondary ecclesial structures, and ministries" (no. 63). It thus involves a thorough rethinking of the gospel in terms and structures resonant with particular cultures, and a focus on the social, political, and spiritual questions and challenges alive in those cultures.

The notions of inculturation and contextualization have since become firmly ingrained in Christian theological thinking. One has come to speak of Latino/a theology, African theology, Indian theology, and so forth, each giving way to even more local or focused theologies, such as Igbo theology, Mestizo theology, or Dalit theology. This raises questions about the relationship among all of these forms of theologizing and about the relationship between the individual and the universal church.

The goal of inculturation and indigenous theologies in the first place is, of course, to better serve the local churches and to respond to their particular needs and questions. But many of the cultural riches mined in the process of inculturation may also become a source of inspiration for other churches or for what is called the universal church. *Evangelii Nuntiandi* clearly warns, "Let us be very careful not to conceive of the universal Church as the sum, or, if one can say so, the more or less anomalous federation of essentially different churches" (no. 62). It implores individual churches to remain in communion with the universal church. But it does not yet fully appreciate the opportunity for the universal church to learn from local churches. There is still an often unspoken assumption that theological models and currents that have developed in Europe remain normative and that local theologies are but various forms of expression of the same theological insights. However, all theology (including Western theology) entails both universal and culturally particular dimensions, and each attempt to express the gospel within a particular culture may bring out new dimensions of its message relevant for all believers. As the center of gravity of the church is shifting, and as the distinction between local and universal or global is becoming more blurred, it is becoming more than ever important and possible for different theological traditions to engage and enrich one another. This is why the department of theology at Boston College established the Duffy Chair in Global Christianity. Each year a theologian from a different continent is invited to deliver a series of lectures dealing with the theological challenges and insights arising from his or her particular context. These challenges and insights may focus on ethical questions, theological developments, biblical hermeneutics, spiritual and ritual practices, and so on. The goal is not only to inform faculty and students of the ways in which theology is done in particular parts of the world but also to raise new questions and offer new insights that might enrich local theological reflection in North America and beyond. The department is very pleased to partner with Orbis Books in order to make the fruit of this theological reflection more broadly available.

The Duffy Chair in Global Christianity was named after Father Stephen J. Duffy (1931–2007), who taught systematic theology at Loyola University in New Orleans from 1971 to 2007, and who was himself deeply engaged with questions of religious and cultural diversity and eager to address these questions in a creative and constructive way. What he wrote about the relationship of Christianity to other religions applies all the more to its relationship to different cultures:

> To the extent that Christianity opens itself to other traditions, it will become different. Not that it will be less Christian or cease to be Christian altogether. It will simply be taking one more step toward catholicity, the fullness it claims to anticipate in the coming reign of God.

Acknowledgments

This book is a fruit of the lectures I delivered at Boston College in 2017 as part of the Duffy Lectures in Global Christianity series. With gratitude to Catherine Cornille, then-chair of the theology department, who first extended the invitation to me to give these lectures, to Richard Gaillardetz for organizing the lectures after succeeding Cornille as department chair in 2016, and to Lisa Sowle Cahill for teaching a course around my talks and facilitating a discussion with her students. I am also indebted to Jeffrey Fagen, dean of St. John's College of Liberal Arts and Sciences in New York, for permitting me to do the lecture series while I was their Visiting Chair of Humanities in 2017; this allowed me to spread out my lectures at Boston College over a period of three months. I also extend my thanks to my Catholic Theological Ethics in the World Church family in Boston, who welcomed me while I was there—especially James Keenan, SJ, Andrea Vicini, SJ, Kristin Heyer, Maria Teresa Dávila, and Toni Ross.

Some of the insights expressed in this book germinated in previous fellowships for which I am grateful: a senior research fellowship at the Center for World Catholicism and Intercultural Theology at DePaul University in Chicago in 2012, and a visiting fellowship granted by the Interfaculty Council for Development Co-operation Scholarships Programme, Katholieke Universiteit Leuven in Belgium, in 2006.

I also recognize the support of the Office of the Vice-Chancellor for Research and Innovation of De La Salle University (DLSU) Manila for this research; Orbis editor Jill Brennan O'Brien and DLSU faculty member Alvenio Mozol Jr. for their help in editing the manuscript; and Robert Ellsberg, publisher of Orbis Books.

Most of all, I am thankful to my husband, Emmanuel de Guzman, and my son, Nathanael de Guzman, for their untiring patience and encouragement as I did my scholarship work!

Introduction

Studies on the development of theological ethics in the Philippines are in a nascent stage. One initial attempt to map the field is the book *Morality of the Heart: Contextualized Moral Theology in the Philippines* by Eugene Elivera with Joselito Alviar Jose.[1] The authors surveyed the publications of thirty-three theologians, fifteen of whom are moral theologians while the rest are theological ethicists who have specialized in other theological disciplines but have written on ethical issues in the Philippine context. Elivera and Alviar's study also looked into themes in fundamental moral theology such as the person, conscience, sin, moral law, and virtues in the local context, and on specific issues that theological ethicists in the Philippines

---

[1] Eugene Elivera with Joselito Alviar Jose, *Morality of the Heart: Contextualized Moral Theology in the Philippines* (Metro-Manila: Paulines, 2013). A general mapping of theologies in context in the Philippines has been undertaken by the Filipino theologian Daniel Franklin Pilario in his essay "The Craft of Contextual Theology: Towards a Conversation on Theological Method in the Philippine Context," *Hapag* 1, no. 1 (2004): 5–39. Earlier mappings include Leonardo Mercado, "Contextual Theology in the Philippines: A Preliminary Report," *Philippiniana Sacra* 14 (1979): 36–58; Rodrigo Tano, *Theology in the Philippine Setting: A Case Study in the Contextualization of Theology* (Metro-Manila: New Day Publishers, 1981); Jaime Belita, *From Logos to Diwa: A Synthesis of Theological Research in the Catholic Graduate Schools in the Philippines (1965–1985)* (Manila: De La Salle University Press, 1987).

xvi • Introduction

have focused on such as reproductive health, martial rule, poverty, injustice, and liberation theology. Their conclusion was: "In sum, the field of moral theology in the Philippines is a relatively fledgling one, but appears promising nevertheless. Compared to the dogmatics sector, that of moral theology remains a largely untilled territory."[2] This book hopes to contribute to developing and systematizing this "largely untilled territory," with a focus on inculturated/contextualized theological ethics in the Philippines. For the Federation of Asian Bishops' Conferences, inculturation—or contextualization in the Protestant circles—is the "deep and mutually enriching encounter between the Gospel and a people with its particular culture and tradition."[3]

Contextualization is as old as the beginning of Christianity. This study on theological ethics in the Philippines, however, will employ a postcolonial lens and will focus on post–Vatican II texts and issues; the Second Vatican Council (1962–65) was instrumental in leading the Catholic Church to a reappreciation of cultures in the church's life and mission. The council significantly affirmed that

---

[2] Elivera, *Morality of the Heart*, 270. See also Dindo Rei M. Tesoro and Joselito Alviar Jose, *The Rise of Filipino Theology* (Metro-Manila: Paulines, 2004), 245–55, which surveyed the works of first-generation, post–Vatican II Filipino theologians. It also outlined the theologians' analyses of Philippine moral concepts and how these compare with Christian morals.

[3] Theological Advisory Commission of the Federation of Asian Bishops' Conferences (FABC), "Theses on the Local Church: A Theological Reflection in the Asian Context," *FABC Papers no. 60*, 18, http://www. fabc.org/fabc%20papers/fabc_paper_60.pdf. A little-known fact is that the word *inculturation* was used for the first time in church parlance in Asia. When the Asian bishops met with Pope Paul VI in Manila in 1970, they reflected, as noted in their final statement, on "the inculturation of the life and message of the Gospel in Asia." Asian Bishops' Meeting, 1970, in *For All the Peoples in Asia: Federation of Asian Bishops' Conferences Documents from 1970 to 1991*, ed. Gaudencio Rosales, DD, and Catalino G. Arevalo, SJ (Metro-Manila: Claretian, 1970), 6, no. 24. In this book, the terms *inculturation* and *contextualization* will be used interchangeably.

the Church, sent to all peoples of every time and place, is not bound exclusively and indissolubly to any race or nation, nor to any particular way of life, or any customary pattern of living, ancient or recent. Faithful to her own tradition and at the same time conscious of her universal mission, she can enter into communion with the various civilizations, to their enrichment and the enrichment of the Church herself.[4]

The backdrop of this more positive appraisal of cultures was the formal independence of many formerly colonized nations in Latin America, Africa, and Asia in the nineteenth and twentieth centuries. Along with this political change, there was an intellectual shift during the early part of the twentieth century from a classicist understanding of culture that regarded Western culture as superior and normative, to an empirical understanding that recognizes the plurality and validity of various cultures. This has led to greater assertion of national and cultural identities, especially for former colonies. This new empirical understanding would be challenged in the latter part of the twentieth century by a globalized concept of culture that is neither fixed nor homogeneous but is instead dynamic, heterogeneous, and subject to contestations of power.[5]

In line with this globalized perspective on culture, postcolonial criticism interrogates in particular how colonial/neocolonial/dominant/metropolitan interests are represented in cultural texts. Its ultimate aim is to decolonize knowledge. The term *postcolonial* is not being used here in the temporal sense, as if colonialism has ended. Although many formerly colonized nations have attained formal independence, other

---

[4] *Gaudium et Spes* (On the Church in the Modern World), 1965, no. 58, http://www.vatican.va/archive/hist_councils/ii_vatican_council/documents/vat-ii_const_19651207_gaudium-et-spes_en.html.

[5] Robert Schreiter, *The New Catholicity: Theology between the Global and the Local* (Maryknoll, NY: Orbis Books, 1997), 28–61.

forms of domination of a state by a superpower or by transnational corporations have emerged (e.g., neocolonialism/imperialism). The "post" in postcolonialism suggests the desire to go "beyond" the colonial in all its manifestations[6] in churches and in society.

Streams of Postcolonialism

Surveying the field, R. S. Sugirtharajah identified three streams of postcolonialism.[7] The first of these consists of textual practices and resistance to colonialism *during* the period of colonization. An example would be Philippine national hero José Rizal's two novels—*Noli me Tangere* (1884) and *El Filibusterismo* (1891)—political satires that exposed colonial and religious oppression in Spanish-occupied Philippines (1521–1898).[8] Although acclaimed in Europe where Rizal studied, they were not widely disseminated in the Philippines and had instead earned for Rizal the label of "filibuster." In the 1950s, however, when the Philippines was an independent nation, the Catholic Church fought against their proposed inclusion in the general curriculum as they were "written by a well-known anti-Catholic,"[9] and they "contain teachings contrary to our

---

[6] Catherine Keller, Michael Nausner, and Mayra Rivera, *Postcolonial Theologies: Divinity and Empire* (St. Louis, MO: Chalice Press, 2004), 7.

[7] R. S. Sugirtharajah, *The Bible and the Third World: Precolonial, Colonial and Postcolonial Encounters* (Cambridge: Cambridge University Press, 2001), 248–50.

[8] José Rizal, *Noli me Tangere (Touch Me Not)*, trans. Ma. Soledad Lacson-Locsin, ed. Raul Locsin (University of Hawai'i Press, 1997); Rizal, *El Filibusterismo*, trans. Leon Ma. Guerrero, 4th ed. (Manila: Guerrero, 2010).

[9] Catholic Welfare Organization statement, January 6, 1950, Pedro C. Quitorio III, *Pastoral Letters, 1945–1995* (Manila: Catholic Bishops' Conference of the Philippines, 1996), 53, cited by Jose Mario Francisco, SJ, "In but Not of the World: Filipino Catholicism and Its Powers," in *Theology and Power: International Perspectives*, ed. Stephen Bullivant, Eric Marcelo O. Genilo, Daniel Franklin Pilario, and Agnes M. Brazal (New York: Paulist Press, 2016), 91.

faith."[10] Nevertheless, their inclusion in school curricula was approved by Congress in the passing of the Rizal Bill, which contained a concession for students who found its content objectionable for religious reasons and allowed them to read edited versions of the text in lieu of the full novel.

The second stream of postcolonialism consists of textual practices and resistance, produced either during the period of colonization or after, and is centered on retrieving the "cultural soul" of a nation. Two major strategies have been employed for this purpose. The first strategy exposes the ploys of the master to manipulate the colonized to believe his claims to supremacy. In the Philippine context, this strategy is illustrated in the essay of historian Renato Constantino on the miseducation of the Filipino. Constantino, who adopted a Marxist-inspired approach to historiography, wrote of the subjugation of the Filipino mind through a colonial-inspired education. English was imposed as the medium of instruction from the elementary school level. Even as other government services were Filipinized during the US American Occupation (1898–1946), education continued to be completely under the occupying nation's control. This education transformed revolutionaries such as Makario Sakay into bandits, and made Filipinos internalize US President William McKinley's concept of "benevolent assimilation" (1898)—this was a policy that alleged that instead of arbitrary rule, individual rights and liberties would be respected and justice observed in the colony. Because of this colonial education, up to this day, many Filipinos gloss over the Philippine–US war and the atrocities committed by the US government such as the introduction of "water cures"[11] and the practice of "reconcentration camps." Constantino remarked, "[American education]

---

[10] Catholic Welfare Organization statement, April 21, 1956, cited by Francisco, "In but Not of the World," 194.

[11] "Water cures" constitute a form of torture in which a person is forced to drink massive amounts of fluid, sometimes to the point of death.

stresses internationalism and underplays nationalism. This sentiment is noble and good, but when it is inculcated in a people who have either forgotten nationalism or never imbibed it, it can cause untold harm."[12]

The second strategy tries to recover what it regards as the "pure essence" of the indigenous soul and culture, which the colonizers had stigmatized. The *Pantayong Pananaw* ("for us-from us" perspective) movement started by University of the Philippines professor Zeus Salazar is classified by its critics under this category.[13] A parallel movement of indigenizing historiography to the Indian subaltern studies founded by the historian Ranajit Guha in the 1980s, Pantayong Pananaw argues against both Marxist-leaning and colonialist approaches to history.[14] From the perspective of the Pantayong Pananaw, the Marxist-leaning approach simply replaced the European meta-narrative of liberalism with that of socialism/communism but remained bound by the influence of Western thought. Unlike the subalternists of India who used the English language, Pantayong Pananaw aims to "construct a uniquely historically contextual Filipino voice," employing the Filipino language.[15] The use of Filipino language is central to the Pantayong Pananaw's goal of constructing Filipino historiography. Proponents of this perspective consider language to be the primary

---

[12] Renato Constantino, *The Miseducation of the Filipino* (Manila: Foundation for Nationalist Studies, 1982).

[13] See Ramon Guillermo, "Exposition, Critique and New Directions for Pantayong Pananaw," *Kyoto Review of Southeast Asia*, https://kyotoreview.org/issue-3-nations-and-stories/exposition-critique-and-new-directions-for-pantayong-pananaw/.

[14] The subaltern refers to "the bottom layers of society constituted by specific modes of exclusion from markets, political-legal representation, and the possibility of full membership in dominant social strata." Gayatri Chakravorty Spivak, "Theses on the Subaltern," in *Mapping Subaltern Studies and the Postcolonial*, ed. Vinayak Chaturvedi (London: Verso, 1999).

[15] Portia L. Reyes, "Fighting Over a Nation: Theorizing a Filipino Historiography," *Postcolonial Studies*, 11 no. 3 (2008): 241–58.

bearer of a people's culture,[16] and are also convinced that discourse can only be truly dialogical when it is intelligible to the Filipino people.[17] While language does indeed express culture, and while it is laudable to strive for intelligibility, this stance betrays a monolithic perspective on culture and grinds against the multicultural milieu of a country with eight major languages and 150 spoken languages.[18] It also fails to recognize that Filipino as the national language has been contested by those who speak Cebuano, which is the spoken language of most of the native population in the country (even though it was not taught formally in educational institutions there until 2012).[19]

The first and second streams of postcolonialism view the indigenous culture as a unified, homogeneous whole, operating within the binary identities of East and West, colonized and colonizer. The third stream of postcolonialism appropriates the postcolonial theory that emerged in the 1980s. This theory is indebted to the collective struggles of writers such as Frantz Fanon and the Subaltern Studies historians in India, as well as the cultural critics of the Birmingham Center for Contemporary

---

[16] Reyes attributes the lesser popularity of *Pantayong Pananaw* internationally as compared to subaltern studies, to its adherence to the sole use of the Filipino language. However, this very principle, in her view, allowed Pantayong Pananaw to continue to survive despite various opposition up to this day. Ibid., 242, 254.

[17] A Philippine theologian who directly appropriated Pantayong Pananaw in her theological discourse is Estella Padilla, in her dissertation, "Ang Mabathalang Pag-aaral sa Ministri ng Pamumuno bilang 'Punong Kadaupang-Palad' sa Katawan ni Kristo at ang Teolohia sa Ministri ni E. Schillebeeckx: Isang Pag-uusap" (PhD in Applied Theology, De La Salle University, Manila, 2003).

[18] "What Language Do They Speak in the Philippines?" worldatlas, https://www.worldatlas.com/articles/what-language-do-they-speak-in-the-philippines.html.

[19] Ammon Ulrich, Norbert Dittmar and Klaus J. Mattheier, *Sociolinguistics: An International Handbook of the Science of Language and Society*, vol. 3 (Berlin: Walter de Gruyter, 2006, 2018).

Cultural Studies led by Raymond Williams, E. P. Thompson, and Stuart Hall.

It is generally accepted that Edward Said (1935–2003) inaugurated postcolonial theory in 1978 with his book *Orientalism*.[20] Said critiqued orientalism, which characterized Oriental studies or what is now referred to as Middle Eastern or Near Eastern studies. Influenced by Michel Foucault, for whom discourse is a way of talking about something at a particular historical conjuncture, Said defined orientalism as a Western way of representing or producing knowledge that is predicated on an essentialist view of the Orient and the Occident and has the effect of restructuring, dominating, and exercising control over the Orient. He noted, for instance, that "in newsreels or news-photos, the Arab is always shown in large numbers. No individuality, no personal characteristics or experiences. Most of the pictures represent mass rage and misery, or irrational (hence hopelessly eccentric) gestures. Lurking behind all of these images is the menace of jihad. Consequence: a fear that the Muslims (or Arabs) will take over the world."[21] In his analysis, Said applies Foucault's insight that discourse is more than just a linguistic concept; it is produced by discursive practices that shape conduct, thus highlighting the link between knowledge and power that is implicated in deciding on issues of what constitutes knowledge, and the regulation of the body.[22] This colonial discourse analysis that Said embarked on would later evolve into what is now known as postcolonial studies.

Homi Bhabha (1949 –), a second key thinker in postcolonial theory, developed the concept of hybridity in relation to the construction of culture and identity in the colonial con-

---

[20] Edward Said, *Orientalism* (New York: Vintage Books, 1978).

[21] Ibid., 285–87.

[22] Michel Foucault, *Power/Knowledge: Selected Interviews and Other Writings, 1972–1977* (New York: Pantheon Books, 1980), 52.

text.[23] Bhabha points out how the colonial government hoped to produce a colonized culture but failed by producing instead a hybrid, an in-between. The production of a hybrid in itself questions any notion of an essentialist cultural identity. Hybridity can refer to the mixed or hyphenated identities of persons (e.g., mestizaje, Asian American) or of texts studying this phenomenon. Hybridity can be linguistic (e.g., Spanish-based creole languages such as Chabacano in the Philippines), cultural (e.g., mestizaje, Asian American), political, and so on. Hybridity in the postcolonial sense, however, is not the same as acculturation and syncretism that may just be a benign combination. Hybridity is a product, in the context of unequal power relations, of both accommodation and resistance to colonial domination. It is in "Signs Taken for Wonders" where Bhabha first wrote of "hybridity" as a tool of subversion that could be used by colonized peoples to challenge different forms of oppression.

Other concepts articulated by Bhabha that are related to hybridity are mimicry, liminality, and third space. Appropriated by Bhabha from Jacques Lacan, mimicry is when the colonized assimilates the culture and imitates (mimics) the ways of the colonizers (e.g., accent, manner of dressing) to gain privileges in the empire. This was illustrated by Frantz Fanon in *Black Skin, White Masks*, wherein he criticized the social pretentiousness of inhabitants of Martinique—who had been to France and who mimic the West—via the imagery of the black man wearing a white mask.[24] For Bhabha, though, mimicry can be unintentionally subversive as when it is used to mock a dominant culture. Bhabha also referred to "liminality"

---

[23] Homi Bhabha, "Signs Taken for Wonders: Questions of Ambivalence and Authority under a Tree outside Delhi, May 1817," *Critical Inquiry* 12, no. 1 "Race," Writing, and Difference (Autumn 1985): 144–65.

[24] See Frantz Fanon, *Black Skin, White Masks*, new ed. (London: Pluto Press, 1986; 2008; originally published by Editions de Seuil, France, 1952 as *Peau Noire, Masques Blanc*).

as the interstitial space where the colonized is in the process of transitioning from or shedding his cultural ways and moving toward assuming those of the white man.[25] Similar to "liminality" is the "Third Space of enunciation,"[26] where cultural statements and systems are constructed. "These *'in-between'* spaces provide the terrain for elaborating strategies of selfhood—singular or communal—that initiate new signs of identity, and innovative sites of collaboration, and contestation in the act of defining the idea of society itself."[27] The "in-between space" is a site for negotiating nationhood, community interest, and cultural values, and is thus also a site of hybridity.

A third major figure in postcolonial theory is Gayatri Chakravorty Spivak (1932 –). In her most cited essay, "Can the Subaltern Speak?" she pointed out that resistance of the subaltern is recognized only when affirmed by the dominant knowledge and politics of a region. This implies, according to Spivak, the need for an infrastructure that would ensure the voice of the subaltern was heard. Spivak also made an important contribution in her critique of the Western feminist universalization of the situation of women without considering class, religious, cultural, linguistic, or national differences. She helped revise feminism to become more attentive to questions of difference among women.[28]

In relation to the Philippine context, a Filipino historian who engaged early on with postcolonial theory is Vicente Rafael. In 1988, he published the book *Contracting Colonial-*

---

[25] The concept of liminality has been introduced by anthropologists Arnold van Gennep and Victor Turner to refer to the transitional phase in rites of passage. See Arnold van Gennep, *Rites of Passage* (Hove, East Sussex: Psychology Press, 1960) and Victor Turner, *The Ritual Process* (London: Penguin, 1969).

[26] Homi K. Bhabha, *The Location of Culture* (New York: Routledge, 1994), 54.

[27] Ibid., 2.

[28] Gayatri Chakravorty Spivak, "French Feminism in an International Frame," *Yale French Studies* 62 (1981): 154–84.

ism.[29] This work looks into the process of translation and conversion in the Tagalog society from 1580 to 1705.[30] How did Tagalog society's reception of concepts differ from or defer to Spanish Christian perspectives? How did such translations reshape peoples' worldview and conduct in a way that reinforces or resists the colonial regime? For instance, Rafael discussed how missionaries often employed the Tagalog idioms of *utang na loob* (debt of inner self) to underline our dependence on God and *hiya* (shame) to render repentance and sorrow for one's sins. Forgiveness was translated in Tagalog as *tawad*, meaning to bargain or haggle, and sin as *sala* or to be remiss in counting. The Tagalogs thus came to regard confession as a means of negotiating one's debt with [colonial] authority, and of avoiding the shock of shame. Instead of confessing their own sins, some brag of the great deeds they have done, or tell of the sins of others as a means of haggling with the authority, a confession without genuine repentance or admission of guilt.[31] Rafael concluded, however, that instead of producing our own brand of Christianity, the Filipinos have never truly been Christianized because they misunderstood the basic Christian tenets. Whether one agrees with his conclusion or not, what he has demonstrated is a postcolonial "way of reading the engagement, transformation and potential transformation of a received message."[32]

Postcolonial theory is basically antifoundational (e.g., in its view of culture, identities, gender) and has been influenced by poststructuralism (Foucault in dialogue with Said), neo-Marxism (Antonio Gramsci with Said), postmodernism, psychoanalysis

---

[29] Vicente L. Rafael, *Contracting Colonialism: Translation and Christian Conversion in Tagalog Society under Early Spanish Rule* (Ithaca, NY: Cornell University Press, 1988).

[30] The Tagalog is an ethnic group from central Luzon in the Philippines.

[31] Rafael, *Contracting Colonialism*, 132–35.

[32] See Bill Ashcroft, "Threshold Theology," in *Colonial Contexts and Postcolonial Theologies: Storyweaving in the Asia Pacific* (New York: Palgrave Macmillan, 2014), 6.

(Jacques Lacan with Bhabha), and feminism (Spivak). Marxism also influenced Said through Fanon and Spivak via the Subaltern Studies Group, which adopted Gramsci's terminology, especially his concepts of "hegemony" and the "subaltern." Postcolonial concerns have since expanded to include the issues of slavery and racism, post-9/11 realities and tensions, globalization, migration/diaspora, disability, LGBTQ (lesbian-gay-bisexual-transsexual-queer), and environment.[33]

In summary, the third stream of postcolonialism dialogues with postcolonial theory, eschews essentialism and totalism, and resists subsuming minorities and those in the margins into a monolithic cultural whole. It goes beyond the binary identities of colonizer and colonized, East and West; instead, its key words are hybridity, liminality, and third space.

Postcolonial Biblical/ Theological-Ethical Reclamations

The conversation between postcolonial theory and biblical studies/theology really began only in the 1990s—postcolonial theory for the most part has ignored faith/religious commitment in its theorizing.[34] As Sugirtharajah noted, "One of the incongruities of postcolonial discourse is that its proponents [Albert Memmi from Tunisia, Fanon from Algeria, and Said from Palestine] hailed from a number of Islamic societies but rarely took account of the potency of religion in these regions."[35]

Postcolonial theology aims to redress this bracketing of religious commitments in postcolonial analysis.[36] Given the

---

[33] See Gayatri Chakravorty Spivak, *Death of a Discipline* (New York: Columbia University Press, 2003).

[34] Susan Abraham, *Identity, Ethics and Nonviolence: A Rahnerian Theological Assessment* (New York: Palgrave Macmillan, 2007).

[35] R. S. Sugirtharajah, "Complacencies and Cul-de-sacs: Christian Theologies and Colonialism," in *Postcolonial Theologies*, 35.

[36] Abraham, *Identity, Ethics and Nonviolence*.

dominant presence of the Bible in colonial conquest, postcolonial theory first influenced theology in the 1990s via the field of biblical studies. Sugirtharajah, Musa Dube, and Fernando Segovia are the pioneers in postcolonial biblical criticism. Among the first cartographers of publications on postcolonial biblical criticism were Sugirtharajah[37] and Jeremy Punt for South Africa.[38]

Sugirtharajah classified postcolonial biblical hermeneutics into three types, namely: vernacular hermeneutics, liberation hermeneutics, and postcolonializing interpretation. This system of classification has also been used more broadly to encompass postcolonial theological reclamations in general.[39]

Vernacular hermeneutics is an approach to inculturation that prioritizes the indigenous in order to de-stigmatize and recover a people's tradition and self-esteem. It generally makes use of any of these three approaches: conceptual correspondence, narrative enrichment, and performantial parallels.[40] Conceptual correspondence aims to find a vernacular term that is a dynamic translation of a biblical or theological concept[41] and can be employed as a lens for reinterpreting the

---

[37] R. S. Sugirtharajah, *The Bible and the Third World: Precolonial, Colonial and Postcolonial Encounters* (Cambridge: Cambridge University Press, 2001).

[38] Jeremy Punt, "Postcolonial Biblical Criticism in South Africa: Some Mind and Road Mapping," *Neotestamentica* 37, no. 1 (2003): 59–85. Wai-Ching Angela Wong was a pioneer in using postcolonial studies to theorize Asian theologies. See Wai-Ching Angela Wong, *"The Poor Woman": A Critical Analysis of Asian Theology and Contemporary Chinese Fiction by Women* (New York: Peter Lang, 2002). Daniel Franklin Pilario, CM, also proposed a mapping of postcolonial theory and its appropriations in theology in "Mapping Postcolonial Theory: Appropriations in Contemporary Theology," *Hapag* 3 (2006): 1–2, 9–51.

[39] See Pilario, ""Mapping Postcolonial Theory."

[40] Sugirtharajah, *The Bible and the Third World*, 175–202.

[41] Charles Kraft, *Christianity in Culture: A Study in Dynamic Biblical*

faith tradition.[42] An example would be the prolific works of translation of the Filipino theologian José de Mesa, such as salvation as *ginhawa* (well-being; ease in breathing) and resurrection as *pagbabangong-dangal* (vindication from shame). Narrative enrichment employs local myths/stories to amplify the meaning of biblical stories. An example is C. S. Song's *The Tears of Lady Meng*, which sees in the suffering of Lady Meng and the "crucified people" the suffering and resurrection of Jesus.[43] Performantial parallels analyze local practices or performances to reveal biblical or theological parallels. One illustration of this is the role of the African trickster as medium of resistance, which finds Scripture parallels in the Hebrew midwives who tricked Pharaoh in disobeying his orders to kill all newborn male Israelites.[44] Vernacular hermeneutics can be considered postcolonial in its resistance against foreign and universalist discourses and its thrust to decolonize the mind.

Liberation hermeneutics, which emerged in the 1960s in Latin America, can likewise be regarded as postcolonial because it criticizes not only the colonial past but also neo-colonialism and other forms of domination. Classic liberation hermeneutics rereads texts through the lens of the poor's struggle for justice. Gustavo Gutiérrez's book *On Job* and Elsa Tamez's *The Amnesty of Grace*, for instance, reread the Bible or do theology from the perspective of the poor regardless of cultural specificities.[45] People's reading of the

---

Theologizing in Cross-Cultural Perspective (Maryknoll, NY: Orbis Books, 1979).

[42] José M. de Mesa, *Bakas: Retrieving the Sense of Sacramentality of the Ordinary* (Manila: Anvil, 2008), xix.

[43] Choan-Seng Song, *The Tears of Lady Meng: A Parable of People's Political Theology* (Geneva: World Council of Churches, 1981).

[44] Naomi Steinberg, "Israelite Tricksters: Their Analogues and Cross-Cultural Study," *Semeia* 42 (1988): 1–13.

[45] Gustavo Gutiérrez, *On Job: God-Talk and the Suffering of the Innocent* (Maryknoll, NY: Orbis Books, 1987); Elsa Tamez, *The Amnesty*

Bible, in turn, highlights ordinary people's interpretation of the Scriptures from the perspective of their issues and contexts. Using their own voices, the "nonspecialist" poor read the Bible themselves through the lens of their current concerns. An example is *The Gospel in Solentiname* which is the fruit of peasants' reflections on the Bible in the context of the Somoza regime (1936–79) in Nicaragua.[46] Later developments are identity-specific readings that emanate from the increasing awareness of the multiplicity of standpoints from which liberationist hermeneutics can be done. Various minority groups such as women, Native American Indians, Palestinians, *dalits*, *burakumin*, indigenous peoples, and others reread the Scripture texts through the lenses of their particular identities.[47]

The third type of postcolonial hermeneutics identified by Sugirtharajah as postcolonializing interpretation appropriates insights from postcolonial theory. Its main tasks are deconstruction, reconstruction, and interrogation of metropolitan/dominant readings toward resistance.

Deconstruction entails analysis of biblical documents, theologies, and doctrines to expose their colonial intentions and subtexts and to bring silenced voices to the surface. To make repressed voices audible, one has to "read like a Canaanite," whereby a reader interpreting a text such as Exodus takes the perspective of the native Canaanite inhabitant whose voice is generally absent in the Scripture text.[48]

of Grace: Justification by Faith from a Latin American Perspective, trans. Sharon H. Ringe (Nashville, TN: Abingdon Press, 1993).

[46] Ernesto Cardenal, *The Gospel in Solentiname*, vols. 1–4 (Maryknoll, NY: Orbis Books, 1982).

[47] See R. S. Sugirtharajah, ed., *Voices from the Margin: Interpreting the Bible in the Third World*, rev. and expanded 3rd ed. (Maryknoll, NY: Orbis Books, 2006), 27–39, 205–58.

[48] Laura E. Donaldson, "Postcolonialism and Biblical Reading: An Introduction," in *Postcolonialism and Scriptural Reading, Semeia 75* (Atlanta, GA: Scholars Press, 1996), 10–12.

The task of reconstruction rereads cultural texts through the lens of postcolonial interests such as past and present-day liberation struggles, subaltern elements in the texts, and concepts of "hybridity, fragmentation, deterritorialization, and hyphenated, double or multiple, identities."[49] For example, Segovia posits that Latino/a theology must start from the hybridity of Latino/a people—their mestizo/a and mulatto/a identity—and should simultaneously stress what the Latinos/as share without erasing the distinctiveness of each group.[50]

A third task of postcolonial hermeneutics involves questioning both colonial and metropolitan/dominant readings to expose the effects of colonialism and/or bring to light resistance on the part of the colonized, the poor, and the oppressed. For instance, postcolonial hermeneutics examines how certain biblical passages (e.g., the issue of taxpaying in Mt 22:15–22) have been interpreted before and after colonization in various phases of a nation's history to show how they have reinscribed and resisted colonial ideologies.[51] The task of resistance also interrogates binary representations such as the backward Orient and progressive Occident; the passive poor[52] and the benevolent rich; and man as oppressor and woman as oppressed.[53]

---

[49] Sugirtharajah, *The Bible and the Third World*, 253.

[50] Fernando Segovia, "Two Places and No Place on Which to Stand," in *Mestizo Christianity*, ed. Arturo J. Banuelas (Maryknoll, NY: Orbis Books, 1995); Michelle A. Gonzalez, "Who Is Americana/o: Theological Anthropology, Postcoloniality and the Spanish-Speaking Americas," in *Postcolonial Theologies*, 58–78.

[51] Sugirtharajah, *The Bible and the Third World*, 257.

[52] Wai-Ching Angela Wong, *The Poor Woman*.

[53] See Kwok Pui-lan, "Unbinding our Feet: Saving Brown Women and Feminist Religious Discourse," in *Postcolonialism, Feminism, and Religious Discourse*, ed. Laura Donaldson and Kwok Pui-lan (New York: Routledge, 2002).

A Liberation-Postcolonial Approach

Sugirtharajah classifies vernacular and liberation theologies as types of postcolonial hermeneutics. Negative reactions to his classification are mostly linked to the anachronistic assimilation of postcolonialism, a term that dates from the mid-1980s.[54] Critics decry the tendency of postcolonial discourse to set itself up as an encompassing theory for liberation and vernacular hermeneutics and for sociohistorical biblical reconstruction. Among these critics is the South African theologian Gerald West, who commented: "Anything particular and local is prone to commodification and consumption by postcolonial theory in general, and postcolonial biblical criticism in particular."[55]

Although it is important to highlight the indebtedness/link of postcolonial criticism to vernacular and liberation hermeneutics, it is also crucial in our view, in agreement with the critics, to preserve the autonomy of these home-grown discourses. For this reason, I shall employ the term *postcolonial* in this book only for those interpretations that belong to the third type of postcolonial criticism, that is, readings influenced by postcolonial theory or discourse, or vernacular and liberation theologies influenced indirectly or directly by postmodern/poststructuralist/neo-Marxist perspectives that have significantly shaped postcolonial critique. All of these theologies have in common the appropriation of postmodern deconstruction, retaining the narrative of liberation, and recognizing the perspectives of the varied "Other."

Two major concerns will be addressed by this postcolonial approach. First is the criticism that postcolonial theory lacks a

---

[54] Arif Dirlik, "The Postcolonial Aura: Third World Criticism in the Age of Global Capitalism," in *Dangerous Liaisons: Gender, Nation, and Postcolonial Perspective*, ed. Anne McClintock, Aamir Mufti, and Ella Shohat (Minneapolis: University of Minnesota Press, 1997), 502.

[55] Gerald West, "Doing Postcolonial Biblical Interpretation@Home: Ten Years of (South) African Ambivalence," *Neotestamentica* 1 (2008): 152; Dirlik, "The Postcolonial Aura."

structural analysis of power.[56] This may be due to the fact that its primary thinkers come from the literary field. Bhabha, for instance, has not been able to theorize adequately on the role of power (and significantly of global capitalism) in the hybridization of cultures. He has been criticized for downplaying the violence involved in many forms of hybridities (e.g., production of the mestizo/a in Latin America) in particular, and for regarding language as the "paradigm of all meaning-creating or signifying systems," thus rendering the "World according to the Word," in general.[57]

West adds that postcolonial hermeneutics has moved very quickly beyond Marxist-influenced liberation hermeneutics.[58] One exception to this may be found in Musa Dube, who remains rooted within a liberation framework, even as she goes beyond it. She clearly refers to postcolonialism as a "servant of liberation."[59] For West, what is needed is for postcolonialism to combine poststructuralism's deconstruction with the theory and praxis of progressive Marxism.[60]

A second major concern is how to redeem the vernacular by fostering vernacular cosmopolitanism. Although postmodern/postcolonial discourses have opened up a space for hitherto marginalized voices to be heard, this has ironically led to the problematizing of cultural identity and thus of the proj-

---

[56] West, "Doing Postcolonial Biblical Interpretation@Home," 147.

[57] Benita Parry, "The Postcolonial: Conceptual Category or Chimera?" *Yearbook of English Studies 27: The Politics of Postcolonial Criticism* (1997): 12.

[58] Roland Boer, "Introduction: Vanishing Mediators?" *Semeia 88* (2001): 6; West, "Doing Postcolonial Biblical Interpretation@Home."

[59] Musa Dube, "Postcolonialism and Liberation," in *Handbook of U.S. Theologies of Liberation*, ed. Miguel de la Torre (St. Louis, MO: Chalice Press, 2004), 293. The anthology *Postcolonial Theologies*, ed. Keller, Nausner, and Rivera, likewise situates the essays within the liberation paradigm.

[60] West, "Doing Postcolonial Biblical Interpretation@Home," 160.

ect of vernacular hermeneutics as well.[61] Even the vernacular cosmopolitanism that Bhabha proposes as an alternative to vernacular hermeneutics has been endorsed very cautiously by Sugirtharajah, because of the danger of essentialism.[62] Vernacular cosmopolitanism engages in translating between cultures and dialoguing with traditions "from a position where 'locality' insists on its own terms, while entering into larger national and societal conversations."[63]

This book proposes to address these concerns by elaborating a method of doing liberation-postcolonial theology that (1) makes use of discourse analysis appropriated from postcolonial neo-Marxist theorist Stuart Hall and (2) fosters vernacular cosmopolitanism that reappreciates the wisdom of the local culture but is also open to insights and intercultural exchange from other cultures.

Structure of the Book

This volume aims to chart the shift in Philippine theological ethics from vernacular/liberation hermeneutics to a postcolonial perspective. It develops a liberation-postcolonial approach in dialogue with Stuart Hall and other social theorists, and critically analyzes certain theological ethical themes from this viewpoint.

The book consists of two parts. Part 1 elaborates on the contextual methodologies employed by theological ethicists in the Philippines and proposes a further development toward a liberation-postcolonial approach.

Chapter 1, "From Vernacular/Liberation to Postcolonial Hermeneutics?" examines the method, contributions, and

---

[61] Sugirtharajah, *The Bible and the Third World*, 175–202.

[62] R. S. Sugirtharajah, *Vernacular Hermeneutics (Bible and Postcolonialism)* (Bloomsbury: T&T Clark, 1999).

[63] Homi Bhabha, "The Vernacular Cosmopolitan," in *Voices of the Crossing: The Impact of Britain on Writers from Asia, the Caribbean and Africa*, ed. Naseem Khan (London: Serpent's Tail, 2000), 141.

limitations of classic vernacular and liberation hermeneutics
employed by representative first-generation, post–Vatican II
moral theologians, and the shift among second- and third-
generation theological ethicists to postcolonial hermeneutics,
even if some of them do not explicitly self-identify as postcolonial theologians. This chapter concludes with criticisms of
early postcolonial discourses, such as the weak link between
cultural discourse and structural dimensions of power (e.g.,
the global economic system), and the challenge posed by vernacular cosmopolitanism's insistence on both "locality" and
intercultural exchange.

Chapter 2, "Discourse Analysis in Doing Liberation-Postcolonial Theology," proposes a way of doing postcolonial
theology via discourse analysis that appropriates postcolo-
nial/neo-Marxist theorist Stuart Hall's circuit of culture, a
perspective that blends philosophico-cultural and structural
analysis while ensuring the simultaneous assertion of local
categories and narratives with cosmopolitanism. This discourse analysis has five components: representation, identities, production, consumption, and regulation. Although Hall
distinguishes culture from the economic and the political for
analytical purposes, the circuit of culture illustrates how
meaning is very much linked with both economic processes
and questions of power.

Employing this discourse analysis as a heuristic guide, part
2 of this book examines ethicists' treatment of contemporary
issues. Essays in this section include constructive theologizing
on vernacular virtues using the method of liberation-postcolonial theology.

Chapter 3 focuses on "Feminism in the Philippine Catholic
Church." Feminist critiques contribute to applied ethics in the
areas of sex and gender and the promotion of women's dignity
and rights. From a postcolonial perspective, sex and gender
cannot be separated from issues of colonialism, authoritarianism, neocolonialism, neoliberal capitalism, and other forms of

domination. This chapter charts how feminism in the Philippines has assumed a strong indigenizing orientation in order to assert that it is not just a Western import but very much rooted in the Philippine historical and sociopolitical context. The key characteristics of feminism in the Philippines include: (1) a shift from nationalist to liberation-postcolonial feminism; (2) dialogue with lived feminist spiritualities in subaltern/autochthonous religious communities; (3) reconstruction of vernacular categories as alternative hermeneutical lenses; (4) the use of narrative theology; and (5) alliance with pro-feminist men. The chapter also delves into the reception of feminist theology in the Philippine Church.

Chapter 4, "Ecological Cultural Struggles of Indigenous Peoples: Toward Sustainability as Flourishing," foregrounds the ecological-cultural struggles of indigenous peoples, and examines how they negotiate their cultural identities and their survival. It argues for an understanding of sustainability as flourishing, which is closer to the indigenous aspiration. The final section discusses the local churches' active engagement in solidarity with indigenous peoples' aspirations toward sustainability and flourishing.

In the context of globalization and the phenomenal speed with which services, information, and capital cross national borders, postcolonial theory has expanded its concerns to include migration and hybrid and transnational identities. Chapter 5, "Migrant Remittances as *Utang na Loob*: Virtues and Vices," discusses remittances within the traditional gift economy operative in Philippine lowland culture; this economy is centered on *utang na loob* (debt of solidarity). The chapter develops a theology of gift based on *utang na loob*, elaborates on *utang na loob* as a virtue, and explores its correlative vices and their roots in neoliberal capitalism driving South to North migration and dependence on remittance. The final section highlights some solidarity initiatives toward virtuous structures.

The final chapter, "Facebook and Populism: Reflections in Cyberethics," attends to the emerging cyberculture brought about by developments in computer-mediated communication. Concretely, it outlines the key characteristics of populism and how social media platforms such as Facebook enable or foster populist discourse—for example, in the campaign and continuing generation of propaganda for President Rodrigo Duterte. It then explores challenges to cyberethics and, in this context, reconstructs *hiya* (shame positively construed as sensitivity to the face of the other) as a crucial vernacular virtue in a digital age.

The Epilogue explores how liberation-postcolonial theologizing goes beyond the "local" as it engages a broader and diversified community of moral discourse.

Part I

Post-Vatican II
Contextual Methodologies

CHAPTER ONE

From Vernacular/Liberation to Postcolonial Hermeneutics?

This chapter examines classic vernacular and liberation hermeneutics employed by representative first-generation, post–Vatican II moral theologians—both their contributions and limitations. It also argues that there is a shift among second- and third-generation theological ethicists to postcolonial hermeneutics, even if some of them may not explicitly self-identify as postcolonial theologians.

Vernacular Hermeneutics

Vernacular hermeneutics makes use of the reader's cultural resources and social experiences to understand biblical narratives and the broader Christian tradition.[1] Sri Lankan diasporic theologian R. S. Sugirtharajah elaborates three approaches in vernacular hermeneutics: conceptual correspondence, narrative enrichment, and performantial parallels.[2] Conceptual correspondence explores a local cultural category that can

---

[1] What can be considered "vernacular" is relative and movable depending on who is using what, and against whom. R. S. Sugirtharajah, *The Bible and the Third World: Precolonial, Colonial and Postcolonial Encounters* (Cambridge: Cambridge University Press, 2001), 178.

[2] Ibid., 175–202.

capture or dynamically translate a biblical/theological concept. Narrative enrichment makes use of vernacular myths/ stories to enhance our reading of biblical stories. Performantial parallels examine similar Christian and local rituals or practices to enrich our understanding of the Christian rituals using local categories. Interestingly, first-generation, post–Vatican II Filipino theologians who do vernacular theologizing have, for the most part, employed the conceptual correspondence approach.[3]

Among the most prolific Filipino moral theologians in the field of vernacular hermeneutics is Dionisio Miranda, SVD.[4] Miranda regards inculturation as a composite of the twin processes of indigenization (what we refer to as vernacular hermeneutics) and contextualization.[5] These concepts have often been regarded as disjunctive but are indeed both concerned with culture, though each emphasizes a different aspect as its essential pole. Inculturation as indigenization focuses on what Miranda calls the "deepest and inalienable in one's nativity."[6] Inculturation as contextualization, in contrast, focuses on context and on how the culture has evolved because of changes relating to other systems such as the political, economic, or

---

[3] This may be due to its conceptual elaboration by leading theologians José M. de Mesa and Dionisio Miranda in systematic and moral theology respectively.

[4] In addition to his articles, Dionisio Miranda's books include the following: *Kaloob ni Kristo: A Filipino Christian Account of Conscience* (Manila: Logos Publications, 2003); *Pagkamakabuhay: On the Side of Life. Prolegomena for Bioethics from a Filipino-Christian Perspective* (Manila: Logos, 1994); *Buting Pinoy (Probe Essays on Value as Filipino)* (Manila: Logos, 1992); *Loob: The Filipino Within: A Preliminary Investigation into a Pre-theological Moral Anthropology* (Manila: Divine Word Publications, 1989); *Pagkamakatao: Reflections on the Theological Virtues in the Philippine Context* (Manila: Divine Word, 1987).

[5] Dionisio Miranda, "Outlines of a Method of Inculturation," *East Asian Pastoral Review* 30 (1993): 151–54.

[6] Ibid., 152.

religious systems. When doing vernacular hermeneutics, Miranda attends to both the indigenous and how these are changing within certain contexts. These two processes of inculturation correspond to the two principal tasks of theology identified by Robert Schreiter: "to help express the identity of the believing community and to help it deal with the social change that comes upon the community."[7]

Perspectives in Doing Inculturation

Miranda identifies the following perspectives that must be taken into consideration when engaging in inculturation.[8]

From Above or Below

For Miranda, although all classes of society should be considered in inculturation, there are historical periods when a particular social class must take priority. In the Philippines, for example, where more than 46 percent of the population is suffering from poverty, he states that inculturation must see the poor as both its "responsibility and resource."[9] Since the majority of the population is poor, this means that the church should give its greatest consideration to the culture of the poor if it wants to be effective in its mission of evangelization. The poor also constitute a main resource for inculturation since, as Miranda asserts, they have been the "principal preservers of indigenous culture," whereas the elite culture has been changing with colonization and Westernization.[10]

---

[7] Robert Schreiter, *Constructing Local Theologies* (Maryknoll, NY: Orbis Books, 1985), 43.

[8] Miranda, "Outlines of a Method of Inculturation," 155–60.

[9] Julius N. Leonen and Philip C. Tubeza, "SWS: 10 Million Filipino Families Rate Themselves Poor," January 17, 2018, http://newsinfo. inquirer.net/960930/sws-10-million-filipino-families-rate-themselves-poor#ixzz5CVYjW9SH.

[10] This does not mean that members of other social classes would no

From Within or from Without

The inculturation process can also occur from within or without, or, put another way, as indigenization or accommodation. In accommodation, "elements that are essentially foreign are so integrated into the culture that they eventually become part of the culture itself," that is, "fully received, appropriated and owned by the host culture."[11] Indigenization, however, starts from elements peculiar to the culture and enhances their growth. Since no culture is self-sufficient unto itself, one must indigenize as well as accommodate ideas from other cultures.[12] For Miranda, this will help prevent nativism, on the one hand, which occurs if one opts to solely indigenize, and abandonment of one's identity on the other, if one chooses to just accommodate.

Tasks of Indigenization-Contextualization

Two important tasks that are addressed in indigenization-contextualization within Philippine theological ethics are: (1) reframing theological-ethical issues in line with the local ethos; and (2) dynamic translation.

Reframing Theological-Ethical Issues

Unearthing the local ethos, Miranda underlines, is integral to inculturation. To use a Western hermeneutic or lens to look at sin or virtue, for example, oftentimes leads to a failure in understanding the local culture.

> Among the very first tasks of inculturation is to determine whether the form of the question, as posed in the Western tradition, is the same form in which it should

---

longer have a role in the task of inculturation. Miranda, "Outlines of a Method of Inculturation," 158.

[11] Ibid., 155.

[12] Ibid., 155–60.

be posed to Filipinos, in view of their culture and context. Does the question interest us (in the sense of touching our fundamental interests, and not merely as a matter of intellectual curiosity)? And if so, is this the form in which it should be articulated (so that it can be meaningfully addressed)?[13]

Because of Western colonialism and claims to cultural superiority, it has been thought that the ethical methodology of the West is the only legitimate way to frame an issue.[14] But Christian values can include traditional vernacular values as well.[15] This point was made as early as the 1960s by moral theologian Vitaliano Gorospe, SJ. Gorospe objected to the denigration of traditional Filipino values such as *bahala na, utang na loob, pakikisama,* and *hiya,* by Western-oriented social scientists who focused solely on their interpretations as "come what may," "debt of gratitude," "smooth interpersonal relations," and "shame as embarrassment," respectively.

In contrast, he stressed the potential of these Filipino values to contribute to Christian renewal. Gorospe emphasizes that the term "traditional Filipino values" does not mean that they are found only in the Philippines; rather, they are universal human values that may assume a different configuration in the Philippine culture.[16] Different cultures may rank, emphasize, or combine values differently. For example, most US

---

[13] Dionisio Miranda, *Kaloob ni Kristo: A Filipino Christian Account of Conscience* (Tagaytay: Logos, 2003), 51.

[14] See Vitaliano R. Gorospe, SJ, *Filipino Values Revisited* (Manila: National Book Store, 1988), 129.

[15] Filipino philosopher Jeremiah Reyes pointed out that the focus on values in the country from the 1960s onward was a result of the influence of the Values Orientation theory of Clyde Kluckholn. See Clyde Kluckhohn, "Values and Value-Orientations in the Theory of Action," in *Towards a General Theory of Action,* ed. Talcott Parsons and Edward A. Shils (Cambridge, MA: Harvard University Press, 1951), 395.

[16] Vitaliano R. Gorospe, "Christian Renewal of Filipino Values," *Philippine Studies* 14 (1966): 191–227.

Americans may value efficiency more than Filipinos, who place greater value on the primacy of the family. These values also evolve through time relative to sociohistorical contexts. After the ousting of the late dictator Ferdinand Marcos in the 1986 People Power revolution, there has been considerable interest in Filipino values as resources for moral recovery. Gorospe emphasizes the need to reappreciate the positive expressions of these values while rejecting the negative ones. *Bahala na* ("come what may"), which is usually represented as fatalistic resignation, can be employed positively as a "Christian sense of responsibility and of trust in Divine Providence."[17]

In the field of applied ethics, *Beyond a Western Bioethics*, a study by Angeles Tan-Alora and Josephine Lumitao, is an example of a reframing of bioethics within the family- and community-oriented Filipino culture, in contrast to the individualist Western culture.[18] The authors point to certain tensions that may arise between the culture and ethical principles, resulting in a modified hierarchy of values. For instance, there is the need to balance individual autonomy and confidentiality (both of which are strongly valued in Western culture) with the role of the family in decision-making processes (which is strongly valued in the Philippine-Asian culture). To use an example from bioethics, a physician sometimes has to play a mediating role if family members do not want to divulge

---

[17] José M. de Mesa would further nuance this insight in his book *And God Said, "Bahala na"* in which he qualifies that Christian *bahala na* is active risk taking coupled with compassion for the other (*malasakit sa kapwa*). José M. de Mesa, *And God Said, "Bahala na": The Theme of Providence in the Lowland Filipino Context* (Metro-Manila: Maryhill School of Theology, 1979).

[18] Angeles Tan-Alora and Josephine Lumitao, *Beyond a Western Bioethics* (Washington, DC: Georgetown University Press, 2001); see also Tan-Alora and Lumitao, "Contextualizing Medical Ethics: Cultural Values and Social Realities," in *Transformative Theological Ethics: East Asian Contexts*, ed. Agnes Brazal, Aloysius Cartagenas, Eric Marcelo Genilo, and James Keenan (Metro-Manila: Ateneo de Manila University Press, 2010), 156–68.

to a patient that he or she is terminally ill; if the doctor is to preserve the patient's autonomy, the family must be convinced of the patient's right to know his or her prognosis. However, the physician also has to stress the value of confidentiality in disclosing diagnoses of patients with HIV/AIDS, since divulging this information to the person's clan may result in harm to the patient and to immediate family members.

Conceptual Correspondence

A second task of indigenization-contextualization emphasized by Philippine theological ethicists is that of translating ethical concepts to the vernacular language. According to Miranda, this task requires both an understanding of the meaning of certain concepts within the local language as a whole that are dynamic and linked to social structures, and a discussion of how a translation compares with its understanding in Scripture, the Scholastic synthesis, and contemporary interpretations.[19] In this task, Western writings or perspectives are considered only as a "comparative point of reference."[20]

As an example of the above, Miranda offered an alternative Filipino translation for conscience as *loobmoral* (moral will, or inner self). Traditionally, conscience has been translated in Filipino as *budhi*. However, *budhi* refers more to the *syneidesis* aspect of conscience—one that accuses a person of the wrong he or she has done ("pangs of conscience"). *Loobmoral*, Miranda posits, is superior to *budhi* in relation to the personalist perspective that retrieves the biblical notion of conscience as centered on the heart or the person. *Loob* is a central concept in Filipino anthropology; it refers to the inner self; the relational will; the heart or font of affection and disposition, feelings, attitudes, thought, decision, and responsibility.[21] It is inseparable from the person and his or her relations. A

---

[19] Dionisio Miranda, SVD, *Pagkamakatao: Reflections on the Theological Virtues in the Philippine Context* (Manila: Divine Word, 1987), 73.

[20] Miranda, *Kaloob ni Kristo*, 74.

[21] Miranda, *Loob*, 108.

person of good character is said to possess a *magandang loob* (beautiful inner self), whereas a person of bad character has *masamang loob* (bad inner self) or *pangit ang loob* (ugly inner self). *Budhi*, in contrast, does not relate to a person's interiority or subjectivity. A person is normally identified with his or her *loob* but not necessarily with his or her *budhi*.

Furthermore, *loob* does not only accuse but also guides in accordance with its fundamental awareness of what constitutes full humanity. It gives not only "negative but also affirmative responses to what should be [*dapat*] in terms of becoming fully human."[22] *Loobmoral* is indeed an alternate translation of conscience that better captures the latter's meaning.

Critical Evaluation

Miranda is a sophisticated vernacular theologian, cognizant of the dynamism and plurality of culture and the various perspectives from which culture can be viewed—from within and without; from above and below. He has pointed out that his approach goes beyond pure linguistic or semantic analysis since a hermeneutics of suspicion is always present in inculturation approaches that move away from Western theological categories.[23] However, his notion of the poor as the principal preservers of indigenous culture shows residual notions of culture as homogeneous and fixed, implying that the latter can be preserved in its pristine state, and is immune from the influence of changing socio-economic-political contexts.[24]

---

[22] Miranda, *Kaloob ni Kristo*, 85.

[23] Dionisio Miranda, "Fragments of a Method for Inculturation," *East Asian Pastoral Review* 30, no. 2 (1993): 177. A hermeneutics of suspicion critiques the manner in which a discourse has been used to promote the interest of dominant (colonial/metropolitan) groups and thus serves to marginalize those on the periphery. See Juan Luis Segundo, *Liberation of Theology*, trans. John Drury (Maryknoll, NY: Orbis Books, 1976).

[24] Miranda, "Outlines of a Method of Inculturation," 158.

For his part, Gorospe focused on the use of positive imagery in countering stereotypes. Although this strategy helps balance the largely negative portrayals of the Filipino value system, it is still working within the binary construction of the Western gaze.[25] Studies on the centrality of *loob* (inner self; relational will) and *kapwa* (fellow; other; together with the other) in the Philippine worldview helped move the understanding of Philippine values beyond these binary constructions.

And although Alora and Lumitao refreshingly address possible bioethical issues at the intersection of Filipino and majority-world perspectives, their underlying concept of culture is clearly that of an integrated whole. Culture, as they have articulated it, "refers to a unified system of ideas and beliefs that shapes a particular group's way of thinking and behavior."[26] Like Miranda,[27] Alora and Lumitao view Eastern and Western cultures through a binary perspective.

Liberationist Ethics

Another form of contextual theologizing in the Philippines starts with liberation as the goal. Liberation theology, which in the Philippines developed in the 1970s as theological reflection on the resistance to the Marcos dictatorship (1972–86), critically engages with Marxist analysis and praxis toward effecting liberation from unjust social structures. Catalino Arevalo, SJ, cites three groups[28] that work along this line: (1) members of the Ecumenical Association of Third World Theologians

---

[25] See Stuart Hall, "Introduction: Who Needs Identity?" in *Questions of Cultural Identity*, ed. Stuart Hall and Paul du Gay (London: Sage, 1996), 274.

[26] Tan-Alora and Lumitao, "Contextualizing Medical Ethics," 157.

[27] See Miranda, *Kaloob ni Kristo*, 92.

[28] Catalino Arevalo, SJ, "Filipino Theology," in *Dictionary of Mission: Theology, History, Perspectives*, ed. Karl Muller, Theo Sundermeier, Stephen B. Bevans, SVD, and Richard H. Bliese (Maryknoll, NY: Orbis Books, 1997), 165.

(EATWOT) and of the underground Christians for National Liberation (CNL), both of which espouse a national democratic vision of social change; (2) theologians who intentionally connect their work with official documents of the church magisterium (in the discussion of this second group, I will include a lesser-known group of social democrats inspired and influenced by Romeo Intengan, SJ); and (3) theologians writing as part of "basic ecclesial communities (BECs) or basic Christian communities," groups that Arevalo notes have "had much influence, especially among the grassroots strata of the church, both in rural and urban settings."[29] I also include in this category other faith-based organizations that advocated for active nonviolence. I discuss each of these groups in turn.

EATWOT, CNL, and the Theology of Struggle

In their opposition to the Marcos dictatorship and their desire to restore democracy in the country, EATWOT and CNL theologians have allied with the Communist Party of the Philippines that has been to this day leading an armed revolutionary struggle.[30] This alliance lasted for fifteen years, according to Anne Harris.[31] Since religion is seen in the Party as oppressive in itself, the theologian members were denigrated as not being genuine revolutionaries because they kept their

---

[29] Ibid.

[30] Victor Aguilan, "Theology of Struggle: A Convergence of Christianity and Marxism in the Philippines," *Asia Journal of Theology* 27 (2013): 153–68.

[31] Anne Harris, "The Theology of Struggle: Recognizing Its Place in Recent Philippine History," *Kasarinlan: Philippine Journal of Third World Studies* 21 no. 2 (2006): 84. See also Diego Quejada on Abesamis's involvement with the National Democratic Front, "A Third Look at Jesus, with Unpristine Eyes: Revisiting the Hermeneutical Suspicion of an Underlying National Democratic Perspective," in Carlos Abesamis, *A Third Look at Jesus: Christian Faith and Social Praxis*, ed. Daniel Franklin Pilario and Enrique Batangan, *Hapag* 10, no. 1 (2013): 47–67.

faith. By 1981, former CNL member Helen Graham, MM, argued that the CNL's Christian identity had altogether vanished, thereby reducing the group to a mere tool of the Communist Party.[32] Theologians connected to these groups who were associated with the theology of struggle include Edicio de la Torre, Carlos Abesamis, SJ, Mary John Mananzan, OSB, Louie Hechanova, CSsR, Karl Gaspar, CSsR, and Virginia Fabella, MM. Hechanova, referring to this theology as *theology of struggle* in 1982, named it as such to focus not on liberation per se but on the people's struggle for liberation. In solidarity with the struggling poor, some of these theologians had been arrested and incarcerated by the military during the dictatorship.

Abesamis described the method of a theology of struggle in the 1970s as a theology done by the poor "or at least, people who by origin or social position may not be grassroots but who are making efforts to remold their minds and hearts to see reality from the standpoint of the liberated grassroots poor."[33] The theologians and biblical exegetes are simply technicians who possess skills and professional competence and are at the service of the real theologians, the poor.[34] This theology, which starts from the contemporary experience and history of the poor and the oppressed, is scientifically analyzed at the intrapersonal, interpersonal, historical, and social level.[35] Alongside the intrapersonal and interpersonal levels (i.e., psychological) are the historical and social (economic, political, cultural,

---

[32] Helen Graham, MM, cited by Harris, "The Theology of Struggle," 94.

[33] Carlos Abesamis, "Faith and Life Reflections from the Grassroots in the Philippines, in *Asia's Struggle for Full Humanity*, ed. Virginia Fabella (Maryknoll, NY: Orbis Books, 1980), 138.

[34] Carlos Abesamis, "Doing Theological Reflection in a Philippine Context," in *The Emergent Gospel: Theology from the Underside of History*, ed. Sergio Torres and Virginia Fabella, MM (Maryknoll, NY: Orbis Books, 1978), 116.

[35] See Deane W. Ferm, *Profiles in Liberation: Third World: 36 Portraits of Third World Theologians* (Eugene, OR: Wipf & Stock, 2004), 73.

and religious) levels. As science is not value-free, Abesamis stressed that "the theologians must know whether the tools of analysis being used are First World or Third World Tools."[36] They employed a Marxist-Maoist analysis as a framework but adapted it to fit the local context.[37] De la Torre explained: "Marxism has to become Chinese in order to transform China. Similarly, Maoism must become Filipino if it is to be effective in the Philippines."[38]

The product of this social analysis must be grounded in the biblico-historical faith, whose core message, Abesamis underlined, is liberating praxis.[39] He identified three ways of looking at the Bible, and Jesus in particular. The first is how Jesus views himself; the second is the Graeco-Roman way of looking at him; the third is the Third World lens, the look from the perspective of the struggling poor. The "third look at Jesus,"[40] he stressed, is closer to the "first look"; consequently, the Bible is better read and interpreted using the Third World lens.[41]

The indigenous peoples, with their millennial history, with their cultural and religious tradition, and recently,

---

[36] Abesamis, "Doing Theological Reflection," 116.

[37] Ibid.; see also Kathleen Nadeau, *Liberation Theology in the Philippines: Faith in a Revolution* (Manila: De La Salle University Press, 2002), 94.

[38] Edicio de la Torre, "The Challenge of Maoism and the Filipino Christian" (1971), in *Touching Ground, Taking Root: Theological and Political Reflections on the Philippine Struggle* (London: Catholic Institute for International Relations, 1986), 67.

[39] Ferm, *Profiles in Liberation*, 73.

[40] The phrase is from the title of Carlos Abesamis's book, *A Third Look at Jesus: A Guidebook along a Road Least Traveled*, 3rd ed. (Metro-Manila: Claretian Publ., 1999).

[41] Carlos Abesamis, "A Third Look at Jesus and Salvation: A Bible Study on Mark 1:14–15," in *Asian Christian Spirituality: Reclaiming Traditions*, ed. Virginia Fabella et al. (Maryknoll, NY: Orbis Books, 1992), 135.

with their own native method of evangelization and their native theology are much better prepared to read and interpret the Bible than the Western European Christian who has a millennial history of violence and conquest, impregnated with the erudite, liberal and modern spirit.[42]

Theology of struggle culminates in actions that transform both the individual and society; to save life, as Jesus did (Mk 3:4).[43] As Eleazar Fernandez, author of the book *Toward a Theology of Struggle*, affirms, "The theology of struggle has accepted the challenge of Marx's eleventh thesis to Feuerbach: 'The philosophers have only interpreted the world in various ways, the point however is to change it.'"[44]

Although their work may bear similarities with the method of liberation theology, some theologians of struggle do not self-identify as liberation theologians. They also do not see that we can create an indigenous Asian theology by using Western theological reflection. At most, Western theologies can only be helpful, in the comparison of methods of theological reflection and in concrete examples. Instead of transplanting a Western tree onto Asian soil, so to speak, the process should involve planting our own Asian tree and grafting only those foreign insights that will help it flourish.

In general, the writings on theology of struggle were not particularly systematic; they were found in works of art such as songs, poems, and paintings, and in communications like letters and testimonies. For some writers, including Harris, the term *theology of struggle* is a misnomer since the term refers more to a movement rather than a systematic theology. More accurately

---

[42] Ibid., 75.

[43] Carlos Abesamis, "Some Paradigms in Re-reading the Bible in a Third-World Setting," *Mission Studies* 7, no.1 (1990): 34.

[44] Eleazar Fernandez, *Toward a Theology of Struggle* (Maryknoll, NY: Orbis Books, 1994), 187.

though, theology of struggle is theology forged on the pastoral and the grassroots level—a level where, as de la Torre underscored, the real theologians are the poor themselves.[45]

Liberation Theology and Catholic Social Teaching

A second group of theologians of liberation reflects on appropriate Christian praxis of liberation in the Philippine context, explicitly in the light of Catholic Social Teaching. As with the theologians of struggle, they may not necessarily self-identify as liberation theologians. They include Bishop Francisco Claver, SJ, Bishop Teodoro Bacani, Jesuit theologians Catalino Arevalo, Antonio Lambino, John Carroll, Asandas Balchand, and Dominican theologian Fausto Gomez.

Some have been tapped as advisers to the Catholic Bishops Conference and have been influential in integrating liberation themes in the local church's social teachings. They have engaged in the task of transmitting Catholic Social Teaching by critically or skillfully applying the church's teachings to the Philippine and Asian contexts. Arevalo was the first to introduce liberation theology in the Philippines in 1970 after his conversation with Gustavo Gutiérrez, Lucio Gera, and Juan Luis Segundo in Latin America, although he rejected the uncritical appropriation of Marxist ideas.[46] He is also a leading theologian consultant to the Federation of Asian Bishops' Conferences (FABC) and was the main author of the FABC I document "Evangelization in Modern Day Asia" (1974)[47] that

---

[45] See also Karl Gaspar, *How Long? Prison Reflections from the Philippines*, ed. Helen Graham and Breda Noonan (Maryknoll, NY: Orbis Books, 1984), 172.

[46] Catalino Arevalo, "A Life in the Service of the Church in the Philippines and of Asia," 13, cited by Pilario, "The Craft of Contextual Theology," *Hapag* 1, no. 1 (2004): 18.

[47] This came out four months before the synod on evangelization, out of which emerged Pope Paul VI's apostolic exhortation *Evangelii Nuntiandi.*

set the course not only for the Philippines but for other Asian nations to engage in a triple dialogue with the poor, with culture, and with other religions.

As noted earlier, other moral theologians connected to this group like Intengan, in contrast, are convinced that faith must be embodied in an ideology, a societal model, and strategies and tactics.[48] They advocate a socialist democratic vision of society, underscoring "democratic" to contrast itself with the more authoritarian national democratic vision of the Communist Party of the Philippines. Intengan is the cofounder of the Philippine Democratic Socialist Party that opted as well for revolutionary struggle during the martial law period. Intengan himself was jailed and exiled.

The influence of Catholic Social Teaching on the various social democratic groups in the Philippines was affirmed by Anna Marie Karaos, associate director of the John J. Carroll Institute on Church and Social Issues: "One undeniable facet of Filipino social democracy is its historical roots in Catholic social teaching and social action propagated by visionaries of an earlier generation."[49]

Liberation Theology from the Basic Ecclesial/Faith-Based Communities

A third group of theologians of liberation are grassroot communities such as the basic ecclesial communities (BEC) and the BEC community organizing groups. The latter

---

[48] See Romeo J. Intengan, SJ, "Christian Faith, Ideologies and Social Transformation: Philippine Experiences," in *Transformative Theological Ethics: East Asian Contexts* (Quezon City: Ateneo de Manila University Press, 2010), 219–37; for the groups that belong to the Socialist Democratic (Socdem) coalition, see Benjamin Tolosa, ed., *Socdem: Filipino Social Democracy in a Time of Turmoil and Transition (1965–1995)* (Metro-Manila: Ateneo de Manila University Press, 2011).

[49] Anna Marie Karaos, "Socdem," 2012, http://opinion.inquirer. net/20767/socdem.

collaborate with NGOs to provide them with skills in community organizing, issue advocacy, and alliance building. These groups may or may not be linked to any of the two groups of liberation theologies mentioned earlier.[50] In their own voices, the members, mostly "nonspecialist" poor, read the Bible through the lens of their current concerns. Their reflections are mainly found in mimeographed papers, songs, theater, and so on. Liberation theologians from the 1960s to the 1980s focused on ethical issues such as the relation between faith and justice, faith and ideology, the role of priests and laity in politics, and armed struggle or active nonviolence as a Christian option.[51] In 1984, interest in the nonviolent option crystallized with the initial visit and seminars conducted by Jean Goss and Hildegard Mayr-Goss, a French couple and leaders of the International Fellowship of Reconciliation.[52] They shared the philosophy of "active nonviolence" (ANV) with members of the clergy including Jaime Cardinal Sin, Bishop Francisco Claver, SJ, and Jose Blanco, SJ, as well as prominent lay leaders in politics. Blanco, who led AKKAPKA (an acronym for the Movement for Justice and Peace that also means "I embrace you"), and Richard Deats on the Protestant side, held seminars on ANV. Trainings were conducted throughout Luzon, the country's biggest island, leading to a coalition of 500 organizations forming an alliance to conduct active nonviolent actions. The theology and praxis of nonviolence exerted a significant influence in the success of the nonviolent People Power that ousted Ferdinand Marcos. Arevalo noted that it

---

[50] See for instance Abesamis's *A Third Look at Jesus*, which is meant to be a catechetical guide for Bible facilitators, catechists, and other pastoral workers.

[51] See Vitaliano Gorospe, SJ, "Active Non-violence," *Life Forum* 15 (1983): 5–12; "The Morality of Protests and Active Non-Violence," in Gorospe, *Filipino Values Revisited*, 233–77.

[52] Ronald J. Sider, *Nonviolent Action: What Christian Ethics Demands but Most Christians Have Never Really Tried* (Grand Rapids, MI: Brazos, 2015).

was the centrist group (and, we would add, those left-of-center politically) who supported this active nonviolent movement.

Critical Evaluation

Without a doubt, liberation ethics has made Christianity in the Philippines socially relevant in the context of the Marcos dictatorship, and it directly and indirectly helped pave the way for his ouster. From an epistemological perspective, however, as with Latin American liberation theology in the 1960s and 1970s, the "struggling poor," the "people," and those at the "grassroots" were generally regarded as a homogeneous whole in the liberation ethics discourse. Theologians and social activists during the dictatorship asked: "Whose side are you on: that of Marcos or that of the people?"[53] It was only after the mid-1980s that identity-specific theologies of liberation emerged that addressed issues such as gender, ethnicity, age, and their intersections.[54] In terms of reading the Bible, there is a tendency to romanticize the perspective of the poor. For Abesamis, to "see things through the eyes of the poor is to see things through the eyes of Jesus."[55] But although the perspective of society's victims (the "poor") can indeed correct the epistemological readings of those in power that function to preserve their privilege in society, the "poor" is likewise not

---

[53] John J. Carroll, SJ, *Forgiving or Forgetting: Churches and the Transition to Democracy in the Philippines* (Metro-Manila: Institute on Church and Social Issues/Life and Peace Institute, 1999), 24.

[54] A significant influence in this direction was the role that religious cultural symbols (e.g., the statue of the Virgin Mary, the rosary) played in the People Power revolution, which called into question the Marxist-Maoist perspective on culture. The rise of women's movements and other identity-specific movements also emerged after the ousting of the dictator.

[55] Carlos H. Abesamis, "Heart of the Matter: Re-Discovering the Core-Message of the New Testament in the Third World," in *Any Room for Christ in Asia*, ed. Leonardo Boff and Virgil Elizondo, *Concilium* 2 (1993): 63–76.

an integrated totality. Furthermore, though these theologians subject interpretations of the Bible to ideological suspicion, they implicitly regard the biblical text itself as free from ideological contaminations. Last, in its desire to develop a Philippine theology and to carve out a space in which Filipinos can find their own voice, EATWOT Philippines in particular has confined its membership to Filipino theologians and excluded progressive foreign missionaries. This might have been necessary in the beginning, but as EATWOT members have gained national and international prominence, is such exclusion still crucial? It can also be asked whether the requirement for a lived solidarity with the struggling poor has unintentionally turned into an ideological check, especially during the first two decades, that led to a narrowing of the group's membership to those that support a similar political ideology.

Postcolonializing Discourses

A number of Filipino theologians have expressed criticisms of vernacular and liberation theologies similar to what we have cited above and along the same lines identified by Sugirtharajah, such as liberation theology's view of the poor as a homogeneous whole; the romanticizing of the poor's epistemological privilege without qualifications; the presupposition that the biblical texts themselves are free from ideologies; the essentialist view of culture; and the privileging of the "insider" perspective as the authentic one, thus tending both to be suspicious of anything that comes from the outside and to overlook a discourse's death-dealing elements.[56] Examples of comparable critiques are found in the essays of Daniel Franklin Pilario, CM, titled "The Craft of Contextual Theology" and "The Politics of Political Representation."[57]

---

[56] Sugirtharajah, *The Bible and the Third World*, 192–202, 239–43.

[57] See Daniel Franklin Pilario, "The Craft of Contextual Theology:

From a positive approach, Jose Mario Francisco, SJ, has synthesized some characteristics of doing moral theology in East Asian contexts that veer away from essentialism/nativism.[58] These include recognizing the hybridity of religious traditions and cultures in general; understanding the contextual location of religious-cultural traditions as lived or practiced; and interacting with social structures resulting in "new negotiated forms on the ground."[59] He also stressed the importance of intercultural dialogue for avoiding totalitarian and dualistic thinking.

This shift in perspective about culture, the poor, and liberation has been facilitated by the contemporary global context in which intercultural encounters and mutual influence have become more common due to great improvements in transportation and communication technologies, coupled with theologians' exposure to poststructuralist deconstruction. In the Philippines in particular, the ousting of the dictator has made it possible to recognize and address a plurality of liberationist concerns. This in turn has paved the way for second- and third-generation post–Vatican II Filipino theological ethicists to shift to postcolonializing discourse that views a cultural text as heterogeneous, dynamic, and subject to contestation, and that views the biblical text itself as shaped by various ideologies.

As outlined by Sugirtharajah and discussed in the introductory chapter of this book, the main tasks of postcolonial hermeneutics are deconstruction, reconstruction, and

---

Towards a Conversation on Theological Method in the Philippine Context," *Hapag* 1, no. 1 (2004): 5–39; Daniel Franklin Pilario, "The Politics of (Political) Representation: Perspectives from Pierre Bourdieu," *Hapag* 1, no. 2 (2004): 79–99.

[58] Jose Mario Francisco, "Context in Doing Moral Theology: East Asian Considerations," in *Doing Asian Theological Ethics in a Cross-cultural and Interreligious Context*, ed. Yiu Sing Lúcás Chan, James F. Keenan, and Shaji George Kochuthara (Bangalore: Dharmaram Publications, 2016), 59–73.

[59] Ibid.

interrogation of metropolitan/dominant readings toward resistance. Deconstruction exposes how colonialist views and interests of dominant groups have shaped the Bible, theologies, and doctrines. Simultaneously, it foregrounds the silenced or muted voices behind these cultural texts. Reconstruction rereads texts in the light of struggles of liberation in the past and the present, hybrid and fragmented identities, and subaltern perspectives. Interrogation of metropolitan/dominant readings aims both to lift up resistance on the part of the dominated and to critique simplistic binary representations. A cursory survey of works labeled as "postcolonial" shows that not all these elements need be present in a particular work for advocates to call it "postcolonial."[60]

Women Doing Postcolonial Theologies

It is notable that most of the theologians in the Philippines who consciously or directly engage with postcolonial categories are women, possibly because of the greater diffusion of postcolonial ideas in international feminist networks and publications.

In her study of deafness and deafhood in Mark 7:1–37, moral theologian Kristin Meneses aims to surface a silenced voice and to interrogate binary representation.[61] She employs

---

[60] See, for instance, W. Anne Joh, "The Transgressive Power of Jeong: A Postcolonial Hybridization of Christology," 149–63, and Mayra Rivera, "God at the Crossroads: A Postcolonial Reading of Sophia," 186–203, both in *Postcolonial Theologies: Divinity and Empire*, ed. Catherine Keller, Michael Nausner, and Mayra Rivera (Missouri: Chalice Press, 2004).

[61] Kristine Meneses, "Welcoming the Other: An Ethics of Deafhood" (PhD diss., St. Vincent School of Theology, 2017) and "Deafness and Deafhood in Mark 7:31–37: 'Seeing/sign World' of Filipino d/Deaf and Their Narratives of Dismemberment and Empowerment in This 'Hearing/word World,'" in *Liberating Power: Asian Feminist Theological Perspectives: Papers from Ecclesia of Women in Asia's 6th Conference*, ed. Jeane Peracullo and Andrea Lizares Si; Kindle ed. (2018).

narrative and socio-rhetorical analysis that pays attention to the signs of resistance or acquiescence to the "hearing/speaking world" both by the deaf and the crowd; she also deconstructs the binary (deaf/hearing) in the text.[62] This narrative has often been interpreted as a story of healing, coming from a medical model that views deafness as a pathology, an audiological deficit. From the perspective of her Deaf community, Meneses uses instead the lens of the cultural-linguistic model that views Deafhood as an ethnicity with a shared language and culture. She further nuances her approach as a "différance model" based on Jacques Derrida's concept of "différance" to stress that the Deaf culture is heterogeneous and dynamic. Building on the initial work of deaf priest Min Seo Park, she shows how Mark 7:31–37 is a story of *ephphatha*.[63] The root word of "open" is *avoigw (anoigo),* with a deeper meaning that is "to cause to understand a thing" or "to open one's soul, that is, to rouse in one the faculty of understanding or the desire of learning." In addition, w = ta *(ota),* that is, "ear" in verse 33, could be understood in two ways. First, the "ear" is literally an ear. Second, the "ear" could be a metaphor, which pertains to "the faculty of perceiving with the mind" or "the faculty of understanding and knowing."

From this perspective, the story need not be read as a narrative of physical healing. Instead, it can be interpreted as an enlightenment of the Deaf toward accepting himself, and thus his tongue was loosened so now he feels free to articulate in his own language. The crowd too was healed of their "deafness" to the d/Deaf who has been wanting to be heard using his own language and to participate in the community.

---

[62] The lowercase "deaf" refers to those who regard deafness as a medical impairment while the uppercase "Deaf" refers to those who consider themselves as an ethnic group with its own shared language and culture.

[63] A Greek word meaning "be opened," spoken by Jesus in Mark 7:34. (Note: for Min Seo and Meneses, the story is not of healing as in the medical model but of enlightenment.)

Meneses, a "hearing" person, reread this gospel with and for the Deaf community where she is considered a member. This is similar to how the South African theologian Musa Dube is making postcolonial theology more accessible and intelligible by broadening the interpretive community to include those whose "suppressed knowledges" should not just be elided by academic theologians.[64]

A reconstruction from the perspective of postcolonial, present-day liberation struggles is Athena Gorospe's book *Narrative and Identity: An Ethical Reading of Exodus 4* using Paul Ricoeur's three mimetic moments: prefiguration, configuration, and refiguration.[65] She identified four significant events in the story of Moses in this text—farewell and leave-taking, migration, attack on a traveler, and circumcision—and elaborated on these both from her perspective as a contemporary reader and from the world of the First Testament. She read Exodus 4:18–26 as an experience of liminality preceding a new identity, status, and community for Moses and his family.

Moses, who is "in-between places" (neither fully Egyptian nor Israelite nor Midianite), bids goodbye to his wife's family to go back to his family of birth. The attack on Moses's life suggests Exodus 4:18–31 as a rite of passage from being a refugee and alien in Midian to a new life with his kin and his

---

[64] Kwok Pui-lan, *Postcolonial Imagination and Feminist Theology* (Louisville, KY: Westminster John Knox Press, 2005), 83–84.

[65] Athena Gorospe, *Narrative and Identity: An Ethical Reading of Exodus* (Leiden/Boston: Brill, 2007). See also Andrew McKie, "Narrative and Ethics in the Literary Hermeneutics of Paul Ricoeur—an Exploration within the Context of Professional Health Care Education," in *Confessions: Confounding Narrative and Ethics*, ed. Eleanor Milligan and Emma Woodley (Cambridge: Cambridge Scholars Press, 2010), 161–80. Another example of a deconstructive and reconstructive reading of a biblical text is Kristine Meneses's "Creatively Claiming Her Space for the 'Other': A Socio-Rhetorical Analysis and Poststructuralist Hermeneutics of Matthew 5:39–41," in *The 21st Century Woman Still Claiming Her Space: Asian Feminist Theological Perspectives*, ed. Virginia Saldanha and Metti Amirtham, SCC (Delhi: Media House, 2018), 206–25.

mission as God's spokesperson. Zipporah circumcising their son symbolizes that Moses and his family had now claimed their identity as Israelites. Because this was a liminal period in which normal conventions did not necessarily apply, it was possible for Zipporah, a woman, to circumcise their son.[66] Gorospe pointed to how this story of Moses the migrant has opened up possibilities for illuminating and refiguring her own experience from being a student migrant to a professional returnee responding to the call to serve, notwithstanding uncertainties awaiting her return—both financial issues and the question of whether she would be able to continue her academic scholarship. The story of Moses the migrant also speaks to other, mostly less privileged migrants facing similar issues of marginality, identity, family, vocation, and community.

Those writing on ethics and migration find it useful to employ such postcolonial concepts as third space; hyphenated, double, or multiple identities; and resistance. In her book *Toward a Theology of Migration*, Gemma Tulud Cruz describes the creative resistance of migrants under strict surveillance by employers. In both Hong Kong and Singapore those who live in the same building transform garbage areas and car parks into "safe meeting places," where the employers cannot monitor them. These become spaces not only for socializing but also for asking for help when it is needed. Creative resistance such as this is part of migrant spirituality, but it is also integral to survival. Migrants are not just passive victims of oppression; they creatively resist in order to transform their lives.

Appropriating ideas from James Scott's *Domination and the Arts of Resistance*[67] and *Weapons of the Weak*,[68] Cruz

---

[66] Susan Ackerman, "Why Is Miriam also among the Prophets? (And Is Zipporah among the Priests?)," *Journal of Biblical Literature* 121, no. 1 (Spring 2002): 71–75.

[67] James C. Scott, *Domination and the Arts of Resistance: Hidden Transcripts* (New Haven: Yale University Press, 1990).

[68] James C. Scott, *Weapons of the Weak: Everyday Forms of Peasant Resistance* (New Haven: Yale University Press, 1995).

wrote of strategies of the oppressed that may seem weak and insignificant but are in fact powerful. Scott calls these "hidden transcripts."[69] These can be in the form of stories, songs, gossips, jokes, rumors, codes, and euphemisms. For example, Jesus himself made use of stories like the parables to destabilize and critique the inequalities in his time. Songs can also express that which is unspeakable. Mary's Magnificat is an example of a song of the powerless that distinguishes what needs to be "celebrated" and what has to be "corrected."

Although not all of these female theologians writing from a Philippine context may self-identify as postcolonial theologians, one finds in their theological works a heterogeneous view of culture and the language of deconstruction, resistance, hybridity, or multiple identities.[70]

Engagement with Progressive Marxism

Postcolonial theory has been ambivalently received in the continents of Africa, Asia, and South America. Among the criticisms is its lack of a structural analysis of power. Gerald West has noted how it has moved very quickly beyond the more

---

[69] Cf. the subtitle of Scott's *Domination and the Arts of Resistance: Hidden Transcripts.*

[70] In the article, "Female Image of God and Women's Leadership in Ciudad Mistica de Dios," I employed Edward Said's contrapuntal reading to show that Ciudad Mistica de Dios, an autochthonous group based in Mount Banahaw, Philippines, is neither Christian nor traditional but a hybrid religion. Borrowing from the field of classical music, Said describes contrapuntal reading as an analysis of two cultural texts in the light of each other with only a provisional privilege given to both narratives. It is like playing two different rhythms or musical instruments simultaneously to yield new music. Agnes M. Brazal, "Female Image of God and Women's Leadership in Ciudad Mistica de Dios," in *Asian Christianities*, ed. Daniel Franklin Pilario, Felix Wilfred, and Huang-Po (London: SCM Press, 2018), *Concilium* 1 (2018): 83–92.

Marxist-influenced liberation theologies.[71] A solution according to West is for postcolonialism to combine poststructuralism's deconstruction with the theory and praxis of progressive Marxism.[72] In the context of the Philippines, liberation theology as an academic subject continued to be taught in some major theological schools even during that time when it was considered "dead" with the downfall of communist-ruled countries. The insights of liberation theology and dialogue with progressive Marxism remain vital for a "two-thirds world" country like the Philippines. In this spirit, second- and third-generation theologians feel free to dialogue with liberation theologies/philosophies from other parts of the world,[73] and with the theories of sociologists such as Pierre Bourdieu,[74] Anthony Giddens,[75] and Stuart Hall.[76] And if postcolonial is to be used

---

[71] Gerald West, "Doing Postcolonial Biblical Interpretation@Home: Ten Years of (South) African Ambivalence," *Neotestamentica* 1 (2008): 147–64.

[72] Ibid., 160.

[73] See Roland Tuazon, CM, "*Pakikipagkapwa* and Its Transformative Potential: An Anadialectical Interpretation," *Catholic Moral Theology in a Pluralistic World, Asian Christian Review* 5, no. 1 (2011): 11–29.

[74] See, for instance, Daniel Franklin Pilario, *Back to the Rough Grounds of Praxis: Exploring Theological Method with Pierre Bourdieu* (Leuven: Leuven University Press and Peeters, 2005), and "The Politics of (Political) Representation: Perspectives from Pierre Bourdieu," *Hapag* 1, no. 2 (2004): 79–99; Agnes M. Brazal and Emmanuel de Guzman, *Intercultural Church: Bridge of Solidarity in the Migration Context* (Borderless Press, 2015); "Interculturality in the Migration Context: Missiological Reflections vis-à-vis P. Bourdieu," in *Utopia hat einen Ort. Beiträge für eine interkulturelle Welt aus vier Kontinenten*, ed. Elisabeth Steffens and Annette Meuthrath (Frankfurt am Main: 2006), 125–34.

[75] Dennis Gonzalez, "New Measures for Justice, Ecological Wisdom, and Integral Development," in *Just Sustainability: Technology, Ecology, and Resource Extraction*, ed. Christiana Peppard and Andrea Vicini (Maryknoll, NY: Orbis Books, 2015), 69–80.

[76] Agnes M. Brazal, "A 'Models' Approach: Teaching Fundamental

to describe this approach, it should be hyphenated or prefixed with liberation (liberation-postcolonial) to underline its liberationist heritage and the need to continue to engage with progressive Marxist thought.

From Vernacular Hermeneutics to Vernacular Cosmopolitanism

One may ask to what extent does this openness to engage deeply with the thoughts of non-Filipino theorists and theologians among relatively younger ethicists help or hinder the development of a Filipino theology?

As an alternative to traditional vernacular hermeneutics, Homi Bhabha proposes a vernacular cosmopolitanism that rejects a binary understanding of the local and the global.[77] Sugirtharajah writes, "It is a discursive practice which anticipates a complicated negotiation requiring an exchange of ideas in all directions, and keeping a constant vigilance over the predatory nature of Western values and treating circumspectly the immaculate qualities of the vernacular."[78] It not only employs a hermeneutics of appreciation in reading one's own culture but also appropriates liberating elements from other cultures. Indeed, this has been done as well by vernacular theologians in their dialogue with the Christian tradition. In vernacular cosmopolitanism however, mutual enrichment occurs not only between the local culture and Christianity but also among various cultures. A vernacular cosmopolitan is

---

Moral Theology in an Intercultural World," in *Transformative Theological Ethics: East Asian Contexts*, ed. Agnes M. Brazal, Aloysius Cartagenas, Eric Genilo, and James F. Keenan (Metro-Manila: Ateneo de Manila University Press, 2010), 69–87.

[77] Homi Bhabha, "The Vernacular Cosmopolitan," in *Voices of the Crossing: The Impact of Britain on Writers from Asia, the Caribbean and Africa*, ed. Naseem Khan (London: Serpent's Tail, 2000), 141.

[78] R. S. Sugirtharajah, *Vernacular Hermeneutics (Bible and Postcolonialism)* (Bloomsbury: T&T Clark, 1999), 38.

engaged in translating between cultures and dialoguing with
traditions "from a position where 'locality' insists on its own
terms, while entering into larger national and societal conversations. This is not a cosmopolitanism of the elite variety
inspired by universalist patterns of humanist thought that run
gloriously across cultures, establishing an enlightened unity."[79]
Vernacular cosmopolitanism has been endorsed very cautiously by Sugirtharajah because of the danger of essentialism.[80] The vernacular, however, remains an important source
of energy for solidarity for marginalized communities. As the
saying goes, "the baby should not be thrown out with the
bathwater." Otherwise, this would leave local or indigenous
communities with nothing but a theology constructed solely
with categories from outside or from the North.

In this chapter I have examined signs of a shift from the
classic vernacular/liberation to postcolonial perspective. Relatively younger theological ethicists tend to think more or less
along the same lines as the postcolonial critique of vernacular
and liberation theologies, even though they may not necessarily self-identify as postcolonial theologians. It is mostly women
theologians who directly make use of postcolonial categories
in their works. Others dialogue with postmodern/poststructur-
alist and neo-Marxists in engaging with the tasks of postcolonial hermeneutics.

In this liberation-postcolonial theological approach, the
non-Filipino discourses have a more integral role when compared with the method of traditional vernacular hermeneutic
and theology of struggle, since these are not just bases for
comparison but are often used as dialogue partners in the
analysis of cultural texts and in dialogue with the faith tradition. The challenge is how to become truly cosmopolitan so
that the local is not erased by the global or the foreign.

---

[79] Bhabha, "The Vernacular Cosmopolitan," 195.
[80] Sugirtharajah, *Vernacular Hermeneutics*.

CHAPTER TWO

Discourse Analysis in Doing Liberation-Postcolonial Theology

This chapter elaborates a way of doing liberation-postcolonial theology that appropriates postcolonial/neo-Marxist theorist Stuart Hall's circuit of culture, which blends philosophico-cultural and structural analysis while ensuring simultaneous assertion of local categories and narratives and cosmopolitanism.[1] According to Hall and his colleagues, there are five major cultural processes—"representation, identity, production, consumption, and regulation"—that "complete a sort of circuit . . . through which any analysis of a cultural text or artifact must pass if it is to be adequately studied."[2] Stuart Hall (1932–2014) was a Jamaican-born cultural theorist who immigrated to the United Kingdom and became one of the founding figures of the Birmingham School of Cultural Studies.

The first section of this chapter discusses Hall's concept of culture and method of discourse analysis, and the second section illustrates the use of this method in systematically articulating and critiquing the theologies of *bayanihan* and *padugo* of the faith-based NGO Gawad Kalinga.

---

[1] Paul du Gay, Stuart Hall, Linda Janes, Hugh Mackay, and Keith Negus, *Doing Cultural Studies: The Story of the Sony Walkman* (Milton Keynes: Open University, 1997), 24–25.

[2] Ibid., 3.

Stuart Hall's Discourse Analysis
—Beyond Culturalism

Culture, Hall posits, is primarily concerned with the practice of "the production and exchange of meanings—the 'giving and taking of meaning'—between the members of a society or group."[3] Hall, however, rejects the static view of culture in culturalism wherein society is understood as a homogeneous and unified totality corresponding to a particular experience: a set of particular political interests, roles, and actions as well as a set of what is considered authentic cultural practice and/or position in the economic sphere.[4] In line with the thought of Italian neo-Marxist philosopher Antonio Gramsci (1891–1937), and in critical dialogue with structuralist and poststructuralist thinkers, Hall stresses the heterogeneity and complexity of societies.[5] Many systems and currents of philosophical thought can thus exist in a given society. Hall emphasizes that a cultural analysis must therefore be attentive to historical specificities and ideologies that shape various modes of representation.[6] In a society viewed as a complex totality, ideology can be understood only in relation to the different levels of articulations (e.g., economic, political, cultural) that are relatively autonomous. Thus no single logic shapes ideology or how people understand their experience. This contrasts with the orthodox Marxist economistic perspective that posits a one-way determination in which the economic simply determines the other articulations.[7]

---

[3] Stuart Hall, Introduction, *Representation: Cultural and Signifying Practices*, ed. Stuart Hall (London: Sage, 1997), 2.

[4] Stuart Hall, "Cultural Studies: Two Paradigms," *Media Culture and Society* 2, no. 1 (January 1980): 57–72.

[5] Du Gay et al., *Doing Cultural Studies*, 12.

[6] Ideology is defined here in a neutral sense, referring to both practical and theoretical reasoning that helps people make sense of their lived experience and social relations.

[7] Antonio Gramsci, *Selections from the Prison Notebooks of Antonio*

Hall's view of representation, as I shall further discuss, not only transcends both culturalism's concept of the social formation as a simple unity but also poststructuralism's view of society as absolute complexity.

Linguistic Turn in Understanding Culture

If culture is the practice of the production and exchange of meanings, language is the primary means by which this occurs. Hall's notion of how language produces meaning can be classified under the constructionist approach to representation.[8] This underlines that it is social actors who construct meaning by making use of representational systems or "languages."

There are two systems of representation involved in the constructionist approach: a conceptual map and a common language. The conceptual map is a set of correlations of objects, people, and events with concepts or mental representations. This system of representation comprises not individual concepts but various ways of organizing or clustering that make use of principles of similarity or difference. A common language is also needed, through which we can correlate our concepts with written words, spoken sounds, or images, in order to express meaning and transmit our ideas to other people. By "language," we are referring not only to written or spoken systems but also visual images that function to express meaning—mechanical, electronic, digital, and so on, and facial expressions or gestures (e.g., fashion)—and sounds such as music. The term *sign* is used to refer to meaning-carrying words, sounds, and images.

Meaning is constructed and fixed by a code that sets up the correlation between our conceptual and language systems in such a way that every time we think of a tree, we use the

---

Gramsci, ed. and trans. Quintin Hoare and Geoffrey Nowell Smith (London: Lawrence and Wishart, 1971), 322.

 [8] Stuart Hall, "The Work of Representation," in *Representation*, 17.

word *tree*. Codes establish the link between concepts and signs. It is important to note that this relation between the sign, the concept, and the objects to which they might be used to refer is arbitrary, thus allowing for the de-articulation and re-articulation of meanings.[9] When a sound or a word is used to symbolize or represent a concept, it assumes the role of a sign and thus *signifies* that concept.

Let us apply this to traffic lights. We share a conceptual map of colors through which we are able to distinguish in our minds the difference between red and green, for example. We also have a linguistic color code whereby we use certain words or images to correlate with colors. There is no natural relation either between *red* and *stop* or between *green* and *go*. It is our shared code that fixes the meaning.

The above perspective on language owes its general expression to the Swiss linguist Ferdinand de Saussure (1857–1913), the father of modern linguistics. Saussure veers away from both the mimetic and intentional approach to representation. In the mimetic theory, meaning is understood to exist and is fixed in the world out there. The intentional approach, in contrast, posits that language simply expresses or represents what an author intends that the words should mean. Critics however would rightly point out that language is a social system based on shared linguistic conventions and codes and therefore it cannot be fully private.[10] Saussure underscores that the production of meaning depends on language. Language as a system of signs is made up of two elements: the signifier and the signified. While the signifier is the form (a word as in the term *laptop*, an image, etc.), the signified is the concept in one's mind with which the form is linked. For example, the signifier "laptop" is associated with a "portable computer," the signified. It is the relation between the signifier and the signified, as established by our cultural and linguistic codes, which makes

---

[9] Ibid., 21.
[10] Ibid., 24.

this representation possible (the association of the word *laptop* with the concept of the "portable computer"). Such a relation between the signifier and the signified is not permanent, as words can shift meanings. For example, "black" (as a signifier) has meant "evil," "sinful," and "beautiful" (as signified) at different historico-cultural moments, indicating that meanings are historically and culturally bound—a contingent result of historical practice.

Saussure further divided language into two parts: *langue* and *parole*. *Langue* refers to the language system's rules and codes, which are shared by users in order to communicate with each other. For example, in English grammar, we have a rule in sentence construction whereby we start with the subject, followed by a verb and then the object—in Latin, however, the verb comes at the end of the sentence. *Parole* refers to the individual or actual speech acts. *Langue* for Saussure constitutes the social part of language whose deep structure can be analyzed because it is limited in nature. *Parole* is simply language's surface and is a fusion of the rule-governed language with the free and creative act of the individual. Because he preferred to study the deep structure of language, people called Saussure a structuralist.

Although Saussure confined his study to linguistics, his theories have been applied to a broad range of cultural artifacts and practices, and this science has been referred to as semiology.[11] Semiology asks: What messages about the culture do these cultural objects convey? The premise here, in what is called the "linguistic turn in [understanding] culture," is that cultural artifacts communicate meaning and, to this extent, make use of signs like language. They can therefore be analyzed using Saussure's linguistic concepts such as signifier/signified, langue/parole, underlying codes and structures, and the arbitrary nature of signs.

---

[11] See Roland Barthes, *Mythologies* (London: Cape, 1972) for examples of the use of the semiotic approach in the interpretation of cultural objects or practices.

Saussure has been rightly criticized for his one-sided focus on langue (the formal aspect of language) which led him to neglect parole—the individual speech acts, and how they are influenced by the status and positions of the various speakers. He studied language separately from the real world that produced it. Later theorists influenced by him, like Hall, would hold that although language in general follows certain rules, these rules can change in response to changing practices. Hall's neo-Marxist sensitivity, in particular, kept him focused on the link between language and specific social, economic, and political practices. He critically appropriates Saussure's model in a looser, more open-ended manner akin to a poststructuralist approach.

Hall acknowledges the importance and—in a sense— the determining pressure of linguistic structure (e.g., shared codes), even as he underlines that these are subject to change.[12] Although shared codes allow for the possibility of dialogue, they do not assure the stability of meaning—especially as different groups further accent meaning depending on their social interests.[13] For Hall, semiology grounds meaning in the text but only partially, for there cannot be a fully objective reading of the text.[14]

Hall's work has been shaped as well by the structural Marxism of thinkers such as Louis Althusser. John Fiske notes that Hall loosened up the "overdetermining relations among the structuring forces of capitalism" as he increasingly moved toward a poststructuralist stance during the mid-1980s.[15] But

---

[12] John Fiske, "Opening the Hallway: Some Remarks on the Fertility of Stuart Hall's Contribution to Critical Theory," in *Stuart Hall: Critical Dialogues in Cultural Studies,* ed. Kuan-Hsing Chen and David Morley (New York: Routledge, 1996), 217.

[13] In his elaboration on this struggle over meaning, Hall integrates V. N. Vološinov's multi-accentual model of language. V. N. Vološinov, *Marxism and the Philosophy of Language,* trans. Ladislav Matejka and I. R. Titunik (New York: Seminar Press, 1973).

[14] Fiske, "Opening the Hallway," 217.

[15] Ibid., 216.

Fiske also maintains that, for Hall, the work of representation (for instance, in the media or in the economy) possesses structural links with class interests, and thus ideology must be understood as structural.

> The constant echoes of the organizing regularities that interconnect systems of representation with systems of politics, of education, of law and order and, of course, the economy are what give Hall's work a footing in the structuralist enterprise (albeit, as we have argued, he seems always poised to step out into the post-structuralist one).[16]

Discursive Approach

Although semiology focuses on how representation can be analyzed by looking at the function of the word as sign in language, the discursive approach shifts to representation's connection with questions of power. The latter coincides more with Hall's rootedness in the neo-Marxist tradition of Antonio Gramsci and the emphasis he gives to historical specificities.

The French philosopher Michel Foucault (1926–84) contributed to this new approach to representation by shifting the focus from meanings to the production of knowledge, and from language to discourse. Discourse, for Foucault, refers to several statements that provide a language to talk about a topic at a particular historical juncture. Discourse prescribes what can be talked about and in what way it can be talked about, and it also rules out ways of speaking or constructing knowledge on the topic.

It is important to note that this notion of discourse does away with the usual distinction between thought and action, language and practice. Discourse here is more than a linguistic

---

[16] Ibid., 217.

concept; it is produced by discursive practices such as institutional rules—neglected in Saussure's approach—that regulate conduct. For example, discourse about madness, punishment, or sexuality can be understood not only in relation to statements about these topics, but also in relation to the following: (1) rules that govern ways of talking about these topics in different but related disciplines (psychiatry, morals, medicine, etc.); (2) the subjects who are supposed to embody the attributes these discourses gave to them (e.g., madman, criminal) and how this supposed knowledge assumed authority as "truth" at a particular historical juncture; (3) the institutional practice of regulating conduct (e.g., "medical treatment of the insane," punishment for the criminal, "moral discipline for the sexually deviant"); and (4) a recognition that in a later historical period, a different discourse will emerge that may produce a new perspective on madness, punishment, or sexuality, with the power to regulate social conduct in new ways.[17] This approach underlines the links between knowledge, power, and the body. Power is implicated in deciding what constitutes knowledge.[18] Likewise, this knowledge has the power to regulate conduct (i.e., of particular bodies), and to restrict as well as discipline practices, and therefore has real effects—thus making itself true. As Hall explained: "Whether the Palestinians are terrorists or not, if we think they are, and act on that 'knowledge,' they in effect become terrorists because we treat them as such. The language (discourse) has real effects in practice: the description becomes 'true.'"[19]

From the poststructuralist discursive approach represented by Foucault, Hall underlined the importance of discourse, the

---

[17] Hall, "The Work of Representation," 45–46.

[18] Michel Foucault, *Power/Knowledge: Selected Interviews and Other Writings, 1972–1977* (New York: Pantheon Books, 1980), 52.

[19] Stuart Hall, "The West and the Rest: Discourse on Power," in *Formations of Modernity*, ed. Stuart Hall and Bram Gieben (Cambridge: Polity, 1992), 293.

links between power and knowledge, the concept of a regime of truth, and how discourse produces certain subject-positions from whose vantage point a particular knowledge makes sense. However, Fiske sums up a crucial difference between Hall and Foucault in the former's hesitation to totally abandon structuralist insights (e.g., the structuring forces of capitalism and tendential lines of history), which he deems important in dealing with the complexities and contradictions of late capitalist society. Some sense of structure and totality is also integral for summoning resistance in terms of a larger alliance and a more global type of struggle. But as Fiske notes:

> Hall's constant return to concrete political and social conditions, his insistence that the real effects of ideology and of representation are material, historically specific and available for empirical analysis would appear to have affinities with more of Foucault's work than he is prepared to recognize. This, of course, is the Gramscian or "culturalist" side of Hall rather than the structuralist one.[20]

Despite his criticism of Foucault, Hall had been greatly influenced by him since the 1980s. Foucault's term *discourse* was frequently employed by Hall.

Method and Theory of Articulation

One contribution of Hall himself to the clarification of the process of representation is what is known as the method or theory of articulation. The term *articulation* seems to have originated with Gramsci, who argued that cultural forms and practices are not simply determined by socioeconomic processes but rather possess relative autonomy. It is articulation that describes how relatively autonomous practices become linked.

---

[20] Fiske, "Opening the Hallway," 217.

Hall defines articulation as:

> the form of the connection that can make a unity of two different elements, under certain conditions. It is a linkage which is not necessary, determined, absolute and essential for all time. You have to ask, under what circumstances can a connection be forged or made? The so-called "unity" of a discourse is really the articulation of different, distinct elements which can be rearticulated in different ways because they have no necessary "belongingness." The "unity" which matters is a linkage between the articulated discourse and the social forces with which it can, under certain historical conditions, but need not necessarily, be connected.[21]

Hall thus employs the term *articulation* in its two senses of (1) speaking and (2) the linking or joining of parts that are not necessarily connected to make a unity. Since there is no necessary correspondence among the elements, it is important to analyze why connections are established at a particular historical moment.

For example, there is no necessary link between women and inferiority or between childbearing and child-rearing. This does not mean to deny how these have been linked in many societies and have formed the cultural and ideological basis of patriarchal structures. In these societies, the "lines of tendential force"[22] articulating women as inferior, or connecting childbearing and child-rearing with political, economic, and ideological structures, are strong. One cannot therefore just separate women from this particular historical embeddedness.

---

[21] Ibid., 53.

[22] Tendential historical relations are not fixed forever. They simply define the historical structuring of a given terrain. Hall, "The Problem of Ideology," 42–43.

"If you want to re-articulate it in another way," Hall notes, "you are going to come across all the grooves that have articulated it already."[23] Texts are not simply free-floating; no text is free of its previous structure of encoding or articulation, or what we can call its ideological history.[24]

These previous encodings can be considered as cultural signposts and traces of past struggles that have marked the various inflections of a text. While not determining future articulations, it is important to learn how to read them if we are to take ideology seriously as a contested terrain.

In his theory of articulation, Hall negotiates between two extremes—culturalism and poststructuralism. On the one hand, in line with a poststructuralist approach, he deconstructs culturalism's structural unity and identity and instead views society as a "network of differences" operating on the micro level. Similarly, the subject is fragmented and decentered. As noted earlier, on the other hand, in line with structuralism, Hall acknowledges the importance and influence of linguistic structure (such as shared codes), even as he stresses that this structure can also evolve.[25]

For Hall, society is a differentiated and complex totality with multiple and contradictory determinations that are historically particular. Each level of articulation or special form of practice (economic, political, ideological, etc.) has its own relative autonomy. This view of society as a complex unity appeals to Hall because it makes one conscious of the need to look at history and agency as consisting of different levels of determination, and it is important as well in dealing with the complexities and contradictions of late capitalist society.

---

[23] Hall, "On Postmodernism and Articulation," 142–43. The example Hall himself gave is on the link between religion and politics.

[24] Stuart Hall, "Reconstruction Work," cited by Lawrence Grossberg, "History, Politics and Postmodernism," in *Critical Dialogues*, 160.

[25] Fiske, "Opening the Hallway," 217.

Articulation within the Circuit of Culture

Hall's notion of articulation underlies his method of cultural analysis. The circuit of culture constitutes the steps through which a study of a cultural text or artifact must pass.[26] It is an approach that is homologous to the outline of commodity production found in Marx's *Grundrisse* and *Capital*. What is produced here, however, is meaning that circulates in a discursive form.[27]

Recall that the circuit of culture conceptualized by Hall and others includes five major cultural processes: *representation, identity, production, consumption,* and *regulation.* I have appropriated them below for use in theologizing.

Representation. Here we ask how the text or cultural artifact is represented in language—is it oral, visual, or written? This step in the circuit of culture starts with the question of meaning that lies neither in the object itself nor in the author, but is constructed. The cultural subjects themselves give meaning to a text or cultural artifact via various modes of representations.

The use of various representational strategies can be explored by considering:

- how meanings have been extended from something known to something new in what can be referred to as the "chain of meaning";
- the expansion of the meanings of a text or an object via an association with various discourses or semantic networks;
- the similarities and differences between a text and other concepts/objects;

---

[26] Hall elaborated on the circuit of culture in the introduction to *Doing Cultural Studies,* ed. Du Gay et al., 3–5.

[27] Stuart Hall, "Encoding/Decoding," in *Media Texts: Authors and Readers,* ed. David Graddol and Oliver Boyd-Barrett (Clevedon, Philadelphia: Adelaide in association with The Open University, 1994), 200.

• articulation with a number of key themes in the broader society.

Identity. What are the identities (based on class/caste, ethnicity, gender, race, age, etc.) connected with such representations? Whose interest does the representation promote? *Production.* Why was this discourse produced? What socio-economic-political structures facilitated the production of the discourse? In relation to *production*, one also analyzes how the meanings various groups have encoded in the text are related to shared conceptual maps or previous encodings. Here we look at the cultural influences in the produced meanings. How is this encoding linked to rules that govern ways of talking about this representation, for example in different disciplines? How can one describe the symbolic power of the groups who produced these discourses, and in relation to consumption, the extent to which their definition has become common sense or a dominant ideology?

Consumption. How are these representations decoded (appropriated / contested / negotiated with) by other social groups? Here we deal with the reception by the consumers or the process of decoding whereby the other person interprets the meaning of a text. People give meaning to things by the way they make use of them in everyday life. They are not merely passive receptors in the face of a dominant ideology. They can accept, oppose, or negotiate the meaning of a text.[28] The meaning encoded in production is not necessarily the meaning received in consumption. We should ask, then, what socio-economic-political structures facilitated the consumption of the discourse? Hall notes that the preferred meaning that is encoded in the text or cultural artifact by a dominant group can "find or clear a space of recognition" in the dominated

---

[28] Stuart Hall, "Notes on Deconstructing the Popular," in *Cultural Theory and Popular Culture: A Reader*, 2nd ed., ed. and intro. John Storey (Essex: Pearson Education Limited, 1998), 446.

classes.[29] To claim that they do not have any influence at all on the "consumers" ignores the existence of dominant ideologies and implies a presupposition that culture can be detached from the distribution of cultural power and the relations of cultural force.

Regulation. How have these various meanings regulated or shaped social conduct? Who are the subjects that are assumed to embody the attributes produced out of these discourses?

According to Hall, the above steps in the analysis of a text or cultural artifact need not be done consecutively; the elements overlap and interact, so it does not really matter where one starts. Each process in the circuit of culture is operative in each of the steps.

This discourse analysis does not separate the philosophico-cultural from the social analysis, for in reality they are inseparable. A cultural text can be a novel, a religious symbol, a social issue, or a political or economic structure. There can be varying representations of this cultural text connected to promoting interests of various identity groups. The inquiry into the production and consumption of a discourse will look into the economic, political, and social context in which a discourse is produced and consumed. Regulation will look at how the discourse affects conduct, including the structures that help sustain this dynamic.

In the end, one has to make a choice from the various representations—a preferred meaning among all the various meanings—of the cultural text one wishes to articulate with a theological concept. This choice is usually based not only on scientific criteria (i.e., the extent to which the representation explains reality measured in terms of adequacy or consistency) but more importantly on ethical criteria (whose interest or what values this representation is reinforcing).[30]

---

[29] Hall, "Encoding/Decoding," 447.

[30] It was Clodovis Boff who concretely proposed the above criteria for the choice of a social theory—the scientific criterion and the ethical crite-

One of the aims of discourse analysis is to identify conflicts or struggles over meaning so as to avoid sacralizing a meaning that reinforces the oppressive powers of dominant groups.[31] It takes seriously ideology as a contested terrain.

Theorizing the Theological-Ethical Praxis of Gawad Kalinga

Gawad Kalinga (in English, "giving care") started out as a social program of the transparochial group Couples for Christ. It hopes to address poverty in the Philippines by transforming and empowering poor communities through its housing and community-building program.[32] Its goal was to build 700,000 homes for the homeless in 7,000 communities in seven years. In 2011, Gawad Kalinga (hereafter, GK) expanded its program to include mentoring social entrepreneurs to enable them to help local farmers and to create wealth in the rural areas.

GK Community Development Foundation and its executive director Antonio Meloto is a recipient of the 2006 Ramon Magsaysay award, the Asian equivalent of the Nobel Peace Prize, for community leadership in providing homes to slum dwellers. GK was also among the thirteen finalists

---

rion. Boff applied these two criteria in the early period of liberation theology to discern, between two different social theories (or representations of poverty), which one of these liberation theologians should dialogue with: the functionalist/modernization theory or the dialectical/dependency theory. Clodovis Boff, *Theology and Praxis: Epistemological Foundations* (Maryknoll, NY: Orbis Books, 1987), 57.

[31] The Indian inculturation of Christianity within the Brahmanic tradition, which was later criticized by other voices such as the Dalits for reinforcing the caste system, points to the importance of discourse analysis even within a certain national culture.

[32] Their program includes: (1) shelter and site development; (2) value-based education for pre-school children and the youth; (3) health programs; (4) *Bayan-anihan* ("Productivity"); (5) GK *Kapitbahayan* ("Neighborhood Empowerment"); (6) Environment; (7) Community Values Formation; (8) GK Enchanted Farm.

for the 2009 Hilton Humanitarian Award, considered the world's largest humanitarian award. In this section, I employ Hall's discourse analysis in theorizing about the theological-ethical praxis of GK, which successfully harnessed vernacular resources to promote housing for marginalized communities. This is a second-order reflection, which means that GK did not itself necessarily go self-reflexively through the discourse analysis. Their reinvention of the vernacular makes sense, however, and can be deepened when it is rearticulated through discourse analysis.

Here, the use of discourse analysis for theology is refined by applying to the various texts a hermeneutics of suspicion and appreciation, from a standpoint shaped by the effective history[33] of the gospels. A hermeneutics of suspicion critiques the manner in which a discourse has been used to promote the interest of dominant (colonial/metropolitan) groups and thus marginalize those in the peripheries. Note that it is not criticizing the culture per se (e.g., Philippine culture) but rather the way a particular cultural text has been represented.[34] A hermeneutics of appreciation, in contrast, is sensitive to how a text has been used to resist colonial/metropolitan discourses and engages in a reconstructive activity that integrates liberation concerns and the active agency of the subaltern or marginalized groups. It retrieves or reinvents the ways in which a particular (vernacular) discourse can be employed in life-giving or humanizing ways.

This liberation-postcolonial method involves mutual listening and dialogue between the local culture and the Christian tradition, and the consequent positive transformation of each in the view of the other. This method also implies mutual transformation between the metropolis/periphery and the

---

[33] Hans-Georg Gadamer, *Truth and Method*, 2nd rev. ed., trans. revised by A. M. Sheridan Smith (New York: Pantheon, 1994).

[34] Cf. José M. de Mesa, *Why Theology Is Never Far Away from Home* (Manila: De La Salle University Press, 2003), 119–23.

dominant/vernacular cultures. It thereby goes beyond essentializing identity and culture (e.g., East vs. West). It further recognizes that the gospel and the local culture are not monolithic wholes and therefore that the dialogue is occurring between multiple cultural orientations.

Discourse Analysis of Bayanihan and Padugo

In the GK discourses, it is not difficult to discern *bayanihan* (cooperative endeavor) and *padugo* (bloodletting) as among the local cultural resources that drive the spirit of the group. A module on *Bayan* (nation), *Bayani* (hero), and *Bayanihan* is given to workers, volunteers, and residents of GK villages. Padugo is often alluded to when describing the sacrifice that volunteers must offer for the cause.

Bayanihan (Cooperative Endeavor)

When Filipinos hear the term *bayanihan*, the first image that usually comes to mind is one of neighbors helping each other move a house, or farmers helping one another during harvest. The context of this discourse is the agricultural rural setting where mutual aid is necessary for people to cope, especially with major agricultural tasks.

Employing semantic analysis, *bayanihan* comes from the root word *bayani* (hero). The suffix "*an*" indicates every person being a "*bayani*" or a "*hero*" to each other. A hero is one who lives and dies for one's country. Modern-day heroes in Philippine discourses, however, include those who bring honor to the country (like Manny Pacquiao)[35] or those who sacrifice for their family and contribute to the nation's economic survival (such as overseas contract workers). Some have questioned the hailing of overseas contract workers (OCWs) as

---

[35] Manny Pacquiao is the only boxer to date who has won world titles in eight different weight divisions or classes. http://www.wboboxing.com/manny-pacquiao/.

heroes. This practice was popularized under the presidency of Corazon Aquino to recognize the sacrifice of migrant workers whose remittances help their families and (importantly, for the government) help their country to pay debts that ballooned during the Marcos dictatorship. Later governments promoted the export of labor to reduce unemployment, but they have not seriously attended to the need to curb corruption in the development of the Philippine economy.[36]

GK ingeniously draws from the nationalist discourse that sees a hero as one who loves and makes sacrifices for his or her country and expands its meaning to embrace a person who "bleeds for the cause," a person who devotes time and resources to initiate work with the community. Here another vernacular concept is tapped: *padugo*.

Padugo (Bloodletting)

Padugo literally means bloodletting. It refers to the animal sacrifice made to ward off evil spirits and to honor *Ginoo* (a traditional way of addressing God). For instance, this ritual is performed at the start of a construction project to ensure the safety of the workers throughout the duration of the project. Among the Subanons, an indigenous group, the ritual is solemnized by a *baliyan*, which is a native priest or a shaman. It is also performed by fisherfolk in Bohol to bless a new boat. The blood of an animal is sprinkled at the helm of the boat to ensure a bountiful catch and to protect the owner from bad weather. The family and friends of the owner then share the cooked animal after the padugo ceremony. Even in the cities, many architects also perform the ritual of padugo (bloodletting) or sacrificing an animal to ask permission and appease the spirit inhabitant in a construction site.

---

[36] One cartoon on the internet says "*Bayani nuon, pulubi ngayon*" ("A hero before, a beggar today"), because when OCWs come back to the Philippines, there are no job possibilities for them there.

Padugo has also been used in protests. In 2015, when the leaders of the Asia-Pacific Economic Council held a meeting in Manila, various protests were staged, including indigenous peoples who held a padugo to drive away the evil spirits in the Malacañang palace—the president's residence.[37] Drawing on the element of "sacrifice" involved in bloodletting, GK creatively reinvented padugo to express bleeding for the cause, or bleeding to give life.[38] Bleeding for the cause may mean volunteering to build a house with the poor, or donating money or land where houses can be built. Sometimes, it is expressed in overcoming great odds and danger as in the case of volunteers who dare to go to conflict-ridden Muslim areas to build houses for the poorest of the poor.[39]

Rearticulation within Christian Discourses

The vernacular discourses on padugo and bayanihan are used as lenses by GK to articulate Christian teachings on sacrifice and self-giving in a more culturally intelligible manner.

Jesus's Padugo

In the Hebrew culture, blood protects life (Exod 4:24–26; 12:27), intercedes (Is 56:7), establishes relationships (Gen 15; Exod 24:3–11), and atones or restores life.[40] This is rooted

---

[37] "Groups Hold Protest Actions Amid Manila's Hosting of APEC," 2015, http://www.gmanetwork.com/news/news/nation/544883/groups-hold-protest-actions-amid-manila-s-hosting-of-apec-summit/story /.

[38] "The Multiplier Effect," http://www.gk1world.com/our-impact; see also "Caretaker Team," 2012, http://www.gk1world.com/Newcaretakerteam.

[39] "Unmaking Poverty," 2007, https://childcareexchange.com/eed/news_print.php?news_id=1735.

[40] Joanne Carlson Brown and Rebecca Parker, "For God So Loved the World," in *Violence Against Women and Children: A Christian Theological Sourcebook*, ed. Carol J. Adams and Marie M. Fortune (New York: Continuum, 1995), 42–43. In the Philippine precolonial context, unlike in

in the understanding of blood as integral to life. It is in this context that the early Christian communities made sense of, or found meaning in, Jesus's death.

In a similar manner, GK makes use of the vernacular discourse on padugo to understand Jesus's padugo—his passion on the cross as the ultimate act of self-giving. Antonio Meloto referred to "Jesus's passion on the cross as the ultimate act of self-giving and the best model of heroism to build a nation. In Gawad Kalinga, we call this brand of heroism padugo or bleeding for the cause—the passion to serve others out of love . . . without counting the cost and beyond self-interest."[41]

Nonetheless, the ethics or spirituality of padugo requires a qualification: God did not will the death of Jesus. Jesus's padugo is not a sacrifice to appease God's wrath and negotiate for our salvation, contrary to the theology behind Anselm's satisfaction theory of atonement. In the satisfaction theory, suffering, "bloodletting," or Jesus's crucifixion in itself is necessary for our salvation. This theological discourse has been used by dominant groups to justify the suffering of colonized peoples and battered women, for example.[42] On the contrary, Jesus's padugo was not a commitment to death but to life, that is, to bringing about God's Reign. With historico-critical exegesis, we now know more of the political milieu of Jesus's time and how his death was a consequence of his preaching about God's reign. It is not a bloodletting that would reinforce or glorify unjust suffering.[43]

---

other cultures, the bloodletting (menstruation) of women, which is important for conceiving life, is not considered to be impure. A blood compact also sealed agreements in the precolonial Philippines.

[41] Antonio Meloto, lecture at Ateneo de Manila University, "I Want to Be a Good Catholic," July 1, 2008, http://couplesforchrist.wikia.com/wiki/I_Want_to_be_a_Good_Catholic.

[42] Brown and Parker, "For God So Loved the World," 40–42.

[43] Referring to the murder of Jesus, the *Catechism for the Catholic Church* 312 qualifies: "In time we can discover that God in his almighty providence can bring a good from the consequences of evil, even a moral

Multiplying Bread with Bayanihan

Meloto made use of the cultural resource of bayanihan (being a hero to one another) to reinterpret the biblical story about Jesus's multiplication of the bread and fishes (Jn 6:1–14). Recognizing the need for a faith-based model for sustainable development, Meloto reinterprets the feeding of five thousand people with five loaves of bread and two fish as the gospel's version of the Bayanihan spirit.[44] Meloto himself did not elaborate on his rereading of this story. But it would have been an equally astounding miracle had Jesus inspired the crowd to bring out their packed lunch and share with their neighbors. With everyone sharing, no one would need to go home hungry that day. This is indeed truly bayanihan! This reinterpretation is also consonant with a postcolonial hermeneutic that focuses on the agency of the marginalized instead of highlighting a unilateral or one-directional empowerment.

Bayanihan and the Pentecost

Bayanihan can also be rendered as a mode of expressing solidarity.[45] The concept of solidarity presupposes that society is a community of diverse elements where all are called to cooperate together for the common good. This call is based

---

evil, caused by his creatures. . . . But for all that, evil never becomes a good" (Manila: Word and Life Publications, 1994); The Catechism for Filipino Catholics 496–497 further explains: "The Exodus liberation . . . is the background for Jesus' saving work as the new Moses. . . . But how did Jesus actually liberate? First, he exposed the enslaving, corrupting power of riches. . . . Second, Jesus taught that any power not rooted in mutual service was enslaving and oppressive." Catholic Bishops' Conference of the Philippines, *1997 Catechism for Filipino Catholics* (Manila: ECCE Word and Life Publications, 1997).

[44] Meloto, "I Want to be a Good Catholic."

[45] See John Paul II, *Sollicitudo Rei Socialis* (1988), 38 (henceforth referred to as *SRS*). http://www.vatican.va/holy_father/john_paul_ii/encyclicals/documents/hf_jp-ii_enc_30121987_sollicitudo-rei-socialis_en.html.

on the fact of our interdependence and our sharing a bond of common origin. Even as the elements are diverse, solidarity involves a deliberate, free choice to join together.[46] The GK bayanihan is a new Pentecost, where people of different languages and ethnicities can be in solidarity with each other for a good cause.[47] In a similar manner, in the GK-led Peace Builds in Mindanao, Christians, Muslims, and indigenous Filipino volunteers have built hundreds of homes for displaced Muslim brothers and sisters.

As Gawad Kalinga transforms into a global movement (GK1World), the new Pentecost also includes non-Filipinos who have been likewise inspired to be in solidarity with the GK communities in helping rebuild the Philippines, or to replicate GK programs in their own countries as in Cambodia and Indonesia.[48]

Evangelization and Nation-building

Nationalism has taken on a basically negative connotation in Europe, largely due to the experience of the monocentric German Nazi nationalism during the Second World War. But in the context of the deeply ingrained colonial mentality among many Filipinos, a healthy sense of nationalism that fosters nation-building and self-determination is not only important but is compatible with Christian discipleship.

GK brings the good news to the poor but also evangelizes the rich by engaging them in their work with the poor and, in the process, bringing them to a deeper conversion. Furthermore, it is not only the rich Filipinos who are called on to help the desperately poor but individuals and groups from all ethnicities and nations. This mode of evangelization cannot be

---

[46] *SRS* 33.

[47] "Gawad Kalinga Transcends Cultural Language Boundaries," 2015, https://thedailyguardian.net/community-news/gawad-kalinga-transcends-cultural-language-boundaries/.

[48] "Southeast Asia," Gawad Kalinga, GK1World, http://www.gk1world.com/global-gk-southeast-asia.

separated from nation-building, according to Meloto, as Jesus himself commissioned his disciples to "make disciples of all nations" (Mt 28:19).[49]

Generating Political Energies

With a renewed understanding of the 'faith rooted in bayanihan (being a hero to one another) and Jesus's padugo (bloodletting), GK taps political resources, opting to embrace the help of various sectors—government and nongovernment organizations, corporations, universities, migrants, peoples of other faiths and nations—to bring about social change.[50] The reinvented discourse on bayanihan and padugo is more than a linguistic concept; it is produced by a discursive practice that includes institutional rules for regulating conduct. GK has organized communities and built alliances that enable people to practice the virtues of bayanihan and padugo in a systematic and institutionalized manner.

Bayanihan Ethics within "Enlightened Capitalism"

An important caveat, however, is that for GK and as clearly stated on their website, "poverty is not an economic problem but rather, a behavioral one. The root cause of poverty is not a scarcity of resources but a deep and painful lack of caring and sharing in our society."[51] According to GK, factors that sustain

---

[49] "CFC and GK," CFC International Council, 2006, http://couplesforchrist.wikia.com/wiki/CFC_and_GK.

[50] GK seems to have been effective with urban poor communities. But with indigenous peoples, it needs to continue to study more their ways in order to be better responsive to their needs. See Martin Perez, "The Myth of Gawad Kalinga: A Profile of the Sitio Target Disaster," 2007, https://mbsperez.wordpress.com/2007/04/10/the-myth-of-gawad-kalinga/.

[51] Gawad Kalinga website, "What Is Poverty Really," January 9, 2010, http://www.gk1world.com/WhatIsPovertyReally.

poverty include "structure[s] that makes farming a discouraging venture," attitudes that alienate people from the land and the poor, and the pervasive colonial mentality.[52] Consequently, GK does not critique global capitalism as a major cause of the deepening divide between the rich and the poor. GK does not engage in political advocacies to change social structures; it does not question or pose a threat to elite class interests.[53] Instead, to eradicate poverty, it seeks to restore the dignity of the poor through decent housing, community empowerment, character building, good citizenship, and social entrepreneurship. The GK Enchanted Farm teaches students from the villages how to farm the land, start their own businesses, and have a positive impact on society. It promotes what it calls an "enlightened capitalism" or a "solidarity economy" that takes pride in Philippine brands, instills bayanihan in place of a colonial mentality, and creates wealth in an inclusive entrepreneurship that does not leave the poor behind.[54]

To achieve its goal of eradicating poverty, and in the spirit of bayanihan, GK partners with people from various sectors including government and business. By being nonpartisan, and by espousing a nonconflictive approach to development, GK is able to get support from the local elite and middle-class Filipinos and those in the diaspora. Its bayanihan ethics is thus circumscribed within the boundaries of an "enlightened capitalist" vision of society. One can validly ask: Does this ethics overcome or reconstitute class differences?

After elaborating on Stuart Hall's presuppositions on culture and method of discourse analysis, I demonstrated how

---

[52] Gawad Kalinga website, http://gk1world.com/gk-enchanted-farm.

[53] See also Faith R. Kares, "Practicing 'Enlightened Capitalism': 'Fil-Am' Heroes, NGO Activism, and the Reconstitution of Class Differences in Philippine Society," *Philippine Studies: Historical and Ethnographic Viewpoints* 62, no. 2 (June 2014): 175–204.

[54] See Tony Meloto, "Skoll Award to Gawad Kalinga: Freedom to Serve," 2012, http://gk1world.com/freedom-to-serve.

the latter can be used in doing liberation-postcolonial theology and criticism, using GK's theological-ethical praxis as a case study.[55] I applied discourse analysis to bayanihan and padugo and illustrated how Gawad Kalinga rearticulated their preferred meaning in Christian discourses. Discourse analysis, as shown, presupposes the multiplicity of representations of a cultural text or artifact as accented by various contexts and interests. It can be employed in theological ethics—if nuanced by a hermeneutics of appreciation and suspicion—in the retrieval, reexamination, and rearticulation of cultural texts (in this case, bayanihan and padugo) within the Christian faith tradition.

---

[55] For another example of doing postcolonial-liberation theological ethics from below, see Agnes M. Brazal, "Harnessing Cultural Resources toward Solidarity," *MST Review* 11, no. 1 (2009): 31–59. Employing discourse analysis, I theorized about the praxis of a Christianized indigenous group (Obo-Manobos) by exploring how they harnessed energy from their traditional practice of dancing. The article demonstrated how this praxis led to cultural regeneration for this group, and to their filing for (and eventually being granted) their ancestral land claim by the government.

Part II

Liberation-Postcolonial Ethics
Contemporary Themes

CHAPTER THREE

Feminism in the Philippine Catholic Church

In 2010, a small group of Filipina feminist theologians from the Ecclesia of Women in Asia (EWA) and the Ecumenical Association of Third World Theologians (EATWOT) expressed their shared concerns about how the growing influence of fundamentalism in all religions, including Catholicism, was threatening to stifle feminist theologizing and erase the contributions and advances that had been made. They saw the need to consolidate forces at this historical conjuncture, and they organized a conference in May 2011 to gather women theologians from different generations to reflect and document the main thrusts of feminist theologizing in the past three decades and its impact on the Philippine Catholic Church.

This chapter draws insights from the papers presented in this conference in charting the historical development, key characteristics, and shifts in thinking and reception of feminist theologizing, particularly in the Philippine Catholic Church.[1]

---

[1] The papers presented in the conference will be published in a forthcoming anthology titled *Roots and Routes: Catholic Feminism in the Philippines*, ed. Virginia Fabella and Agnes M. Brazal (Metro-Manila: Claretian Publications).

Historical Background

The beginnings of feminism in the country can be traced to the twenty women of Malolos—a town near Manila—who sent a letter in 1888 to the Spanish Governor-General asking if they could have an evening school where they could learn the Spanish language. More than a request, this could be read as a demand for equal rights, a challenge to prevailing norms. The women wanted to learn Spanish, which was the language of politics at the time. The request was eventually granted even if in the beginning it was blocked by the Spanish friar of Malolos, who saw it as a threat to the government.[2]

In 1905, ten of the women of Malolos founded the Asociacion Feminista Filipina. Together with the Asociacion Feminista Ilonga formed in 1906, this constituted the backbone of the suffragist movement that lobbied for Filipino women's right to vote in the 1920s and 1930s. Having won that right in 1937, they made the Filipinas the first women in Asia to gain the right to vote, and among the earliest in the two-thirds or majority world to attain this goal.[3]

The true flowering of the women's movement in the Philippines, however, would occur in the 1980s, especially after the 1986 People Power revolution that toppled the Marcos dictatorship. These revolutionary groups resisted the dictatorship, sex tourism, prostitution, the US military bases in the Philippines, and more. PILIPINA, which formed in 1980, was the first self-identified feminist group in this period that tackled "women's issues" such as media sexism, violence against women, prostitution, and reproductive rights.[4] Before this,

---

[2] Quennie Ann J. Palafox, "Girl Power: The Women of Malolos," National Historical Commission of the Philippines, 2012, http://nhcp. gov.ph/girl-power-the-women-of-malolos/.

[3] Lilia Quindoza-Santiago, "Roots of Feminist Thought in the Philippines," 1996, 168, www.journals.upd.edu.ph/index.php/rws/article/viewFile/3112/2929.

[4] Carolyn Sobritchea, "Women's Movement in the Philippines and

gender issues were either grudgingly acknowledged or subordinated to the national struggle for sovereignty. PILIPINA was formed by women who were former leaders of social action centers in different dioceses and other church-based institutions.[5] In 1984, national democratic activists formed GABRIELA (General Assembly Binding Women for Reforms, Integrity, Equality and Action) as a coalition of women's organizations. This group was at first focused more on advocating for the dismantling of the dictatorship and for justice for human rights victims.[6]

A major push toward the development of feminist theologizing was the Second Vatican Council, which emphasized the need for theological education for women religious and laypeople. From this group of theologically educated women emerged the first generation of Filipina feminist theologians. Feminist theological writings began to be published in the mid-1980s, beginning with Mary John Mananzan's *Essays on Women*, which dealt with the development of women's movements in the Philippines.[7]

Most first-generation feminist theologians began as social activists engaged in the struggle to dismantle the dictatorship; they then expanded their concerns to integrate feminist issues. This group of theologians would include members of the EAT-WOT Philippines, who were associated with the theology of

---

the Politics of Critical Collaboration with the State," in *Civil Society in Southeast Asia*, ed. L. H. Guan (Singapore and Copenhagen: ISEAS and NIAS Press), 103.

[5] Interview with Eleanor Dionisio, associate director, John J. Carroll Institute on Church and Social Issues.

[6] Aurora Javate De Dios, "Converging Paths: Women's Movement and Women's Studies in Philippines," in *Roots and Routes*, ed. Fabella and Brazal.

[7] Mary John Mananzan, OSB, ed., *Essays on Women* (Manila: St. Scholastica's College, 1987).

struggle.[8] The theology of struggle had developed more than a decade earlier as theological reflection on the resistance to the fourteen-year Marcos dictatorship (1972–1986), critically engaging with Marxist-Maoist analysis and praxis toward effecting liberation from unjust social structures.

As members of EATWOT International, some Filipina theologians were present in what Mercy Amba Oduyoye, a Methodist theologian from Ghana, calls the "irruption within the irruption of the poor in the third world."[9] This refers to the intervention of the EATWOT women in their 1981 conference, against the gender-blindness and sexism within the organization itself of supposedly progressive theologians. They made the third world male theologians aware that sexism should not be simply dismissed as the grumblings of a few discontented women, but an oppression that needed to be seriously addressed. This led to the formation of the Women's Commission in the succeeding EATWOT conference in Geneva in 1983. The national and Asian regional consultations held in the succeeding years stimulated the growth of feminist theologizing in the Philippines.

Likewise, the publication of *In God's Image* by the Asian Women's Resource Center for Culture and Theology, founded in 1987 in Singapore, provided women theologians in Asia a forum for their feminist writings.

From the 1990s onward, women theologians who finished their doctorates in theology abroad had returned, and together with feminist foreign missionaries would strengthen the presence of feminist theologies in major theological schools in Manila.

The start of the third millennium also saw the emergence of other theological associations, both local and regional, which have provided support to feminist theologizing in the Phil-

---

[8] See Chapter 1.

[9] Virginia Fabella, *Beyond Bonding: A Third World Women's Theological Journey* (Manila: EATWOT, 1993), 93.

ippines. These include the Ecclesia of Women in Asia (EWA) formed in November 2002 in Bangkok, Thailand:

> Its mission is to encourage Catholic women in particular to engage in research, reflection and writing from an Asian feminist perspective toward doing theology that: (1) is inculturated and contextualized in Asian realities; (2) is built on the religious experience and praxis of the socially excluded; (3) promotes gender mutuality and the integrity of creation; and (4) fosters dialogue with other disciplines and faiths.[10]

Its biennial anthologies have promoted publications on women's issues from the Philippines. On the local level, the Catholic Biblical Association of the Philippines was founded in 2000, with two women scripture scholars as founding members— Ma. Anicia Co, RVM, and Niceta M. Vargas, OSA. That organization encouraged different approaches and methodologies in biblical interpretation, including feminist biblical hermeneutics. Similarly, in 2002, the Catholic Theological Society of the Philippines (Damdaming Katoliko sa Teolohiya) was formed with Agnes M. Brazal as co-founding member. Contextualized theological articles, which include feminist discourses, are included annually in an issue of the *Hapag* journal.

The Problem of Naming

The term *feminist* has been a difficult one to embrace for Filipino women theologians because of its white, Western, and middle-class origins, its association with man-hating, and the impression that feminists are angry and aggressive women even as local theologians do not hesitate to show their militant faces in protest rallies and demonstrations. They prefer

---

[10] See Agnes M. Brazal and Andrea Lizares-Si, eds., *Body and Sexuality: Theological-Pastoral Perspectives of Women in Asia* (Manila: Ateneo de Manila University Press, 2007), viii.

the terms *inclusive* or *gender-sensitive*, while those active in the environmental movement prefer the label *ecofeminist*. There is a strong minority though who do not mind being called feminist if this refers to one working with women to promote their rights, empowerment, and protection against violence and discrimination. They emphasize that its meaning is evolving and depends on its dynamic social construction.[11]

In the gathering of feminist theologians in May 2011, the name *Bai* or *Bae* was raised as an alternative and gained the most approval. *Bai* is an honorific title for a woman tribal leader among the indigenous groups (lumads) in the South [Mindanao].[12] It is also the root word for *woman* in various languages in the country. Since bai connotes a strong woman who can equally become a leader in the community, the group saw it as a fitting term to name Philippine feminist theologizing.

Key Characteristics of Bai Theology

Bai theology is doing theology from the perspective of women's struggle for liberation in the Philippine and transnational context.

From Nationalist to Liberation-Postcolonial Feminism

Because of the Philippines' colonial history, women activists are "conscious about not merely grafting Western feminist ideologies onto the Philippine context."[13] Suffragists of the early

---

[11] Agnes M. Brazal and Arche Ligo, "Bai Theology: Present and Future Directions," in *Roots and Routes: Catholic Feminism in the Philippines*, ed. Fabella and Brazal.

[12] Ronalyn V. Olea, "Bai Bigkay Biyaon: A Woman Tribe Leader Ready to Die for Her Land," 2012, http://bulatlat.com/main/2012/12/06/bai-bigkay-biyaon-a-woman-tribe-leader-ready-to-die-for-her-land/.

[13] Mina Roces, "Rethinking 'the Filipino Woman': A Century of Women's Activism in the Philippines, 1905–2006," in *Women's Movements in*

twentieth century were accused of simply imitating US American women in their desire to vote and run for political office. As with the broader Philippine feminist movement, bai theologians stressed the primacy of the Philippine context, and of producing their "own brand of 'homegrown' feminism." This uneasy relationship with Western feminism compels the search for the Filipino response to how womanhood has been defined by culture, religion, history, and the colonial and imperialist experience.[14] As Bai theologian Carmelita Usog writes, "It is important to craft our own theory—nationalist feminism that addresses both the 'colonial question' and the 'woman question.'"[15]

In 1970, the group MAKIBAKA (Malayang Kilusan ng Bagong Kababaihan, or Free Movement of New Women) was formed to address specifically the discrimination and exploitation of women within the context of the struggle for national liberation. The split between nationalism and feminism persisted in the movement, however, because most members, following a Marxist historical materialist perspective, subordinated gender to nationalist concerns. The movement met an early demise with the declaration of martial law in 1972. MAKIBAKA founder Maria Lorena Barros nevertheless had already created feminist stirrings toward the eventual formation of feminist groups such as PILIPINA and later GABRIELA in the 1980s, which would incorporate the role of patriarchy in its analysis of women's oppression. For Usog, nationalist feminism remains relevant as it responds both to the "woman question" and the "colonial question" we currently experience in the form of neocolonialism or imperialism.[16]

Asia: Feminism and Transnational Activism, ed. Mina Roces and Louise Edwards (New York: Routledge, 2010), 39.

[14] Mina Roces, "Asian Feminisms: Women's Movements from the Asian Perspective," in *Women's Movements in Asia*, ed. Roces and Edwards, 2.

[15] Carmelita Usog, "Nationalist Feminism: Erasing the Dichotomy," in *Roots and Routes*.

[16] The tension between the "woman question" and the "colonial

The concept of "coloniality" has expanded since the 1980s to include other forms of domination, such as ethnocentrism. Second- and third-generation bai theologians now speak more of the postcolonial instead of the more restrictive nationalist feminism. Both in the migration context and within the country, postcolonial bai theologizing entails interrogating gender as it intersects with colonialism/neocolonialism, neoliberalism, ethnocentrism, racism, and so on.

Postcolonial feminism in the Philippines shares the view with nationalist feminism that even as the country has gained independence from colonial powers, it continues to bear the negative impact of (1) neocolonial policies; (2) a deep-seated colonial mentality among Filipinos; and (3) an underdeveloped sense of nationhood. In a postcolonial perspective, however, this nationalist discourse needs to be problematized in light of the existence, for instance, of the Bangsamoro or the Moro nation in Southern Philippines. Bai theologians have not had formal dialogues with Muslim feminists in the South, as they have with the secular feminists. At the very least, however, on the theoretical level, the concept of nationalism has to be reconsidered in light of the existence of other nations within the State.

In the context of globalization and migration where intercultural exchange is heightened, postcolonial bai theologians, unlike their predecessors, are more open to appropriating foreign theories and discourses. They need to be cognizant,

---

question" dates back to the colonial times when the suffragists had to campaign first for the ratification of the 1934 Philippine Constitution (which actually opposed women's suffrage, but emphasized Philippine independence from the US American colonizers), before they could focus on the issue of the women's vote. See Usog, "Nationalist Feminism." Historian Mina Roces described in the book *Women's Movements in Asia* the development of a national-essence feminism not only in the Philippines but also in the whole of Asia. See Mina Roces, "Asian Feminisms," in *Women's Movements in Asia*, 4.

however, of the asymmetrical relationships in the production of global knowledge and thus the need to maintain, if not strengthen, feminist hermeneutics of appreciation for vernacular discourses. As people continue to develop their thoughts and frameworks, the line dividing national "essence" feminists and postcolonial feminists is blurred. Feminists are more sensitive to the role of power, particularly patriarchal power, in the construction of culture, and thus are less likely to regard culture as a homogeneous whole.

Reconstructing Vernacular Feminist Elements

In line with the thrust toward a homegrown feminism, feminist theologians turned to indigenous cultures and popular religiosity. But among some bai theologians, this shift did not happen until after the 1986 People Power or EDSA Revolution. The People Power surprised those who were holding on to a rigid Marxist analysis that looked down on popular religiosity; and in the EDSA revolution, they witnessed the power of cultural and religious symbols, such as statues of the Virgin Mary and the Rosary, to deter the military from firing at people.[17] The turn to cultural analysis in the Philippines was not brought about primarily by postmodern ideas but was facilitated instead by the 1986 People Power Revolution.

As the EATWOT theologians (including Virginia Fabella, Arche Ligo, Rosario Battung, and Elizabeth Tapia) reported in the third Asian Christian Theological Conference in Korea (1991),

---

[17] See Christina Astorga, "Culture, Religion, and Moral Discourse: A Theological Discourse on the Filipino People Power Revolution of 1986," *Theological Studies* (2006): 567–601, and the caveat of Randy J. C. Odchigue on her reading of the People Power revolution, which elided the political dynamics at work in EDSA, in "Church *Power,* People *Power:* Hegemonies and Resistances," in *Theology and Power: International Perspectives*, ed. Stephen Bullivant, Eric Marcelo O. Genilo, Daniel Franklin Pilario, and Agnes M. Brazal (Mahwah, N.J.: Paulist Press, 2016), 106.

In general most of us had a condescending attitude toward the popular beliefs and practices of our people, seeing no connection between them and the liberating work of Jesus. Many of us saw them as superstitious, remnants of old traditional beliefs, which served as obstacles to the process of politicization and the people's struggle for liberation.[18]

This conversion toward greater appreciation of popular and indigenous culture as sources of empowerment in justice and peace efforts would shape the later direction of bai theologizing.

Babaylan as Iconic Model

In the search for alternative models of womanhood, feminists now turned to the precolonial past to retrieve the figure of the *babaylan.* Fe Mangahas, a bai historian, writes of the seeds of feminism in babaylanism.[19] The precolonial babaylan, who were mostly female, were the religious leaders. Together with the male war leaders (*datu*) and the male blacksmiths (*panday*), the babaylan led the community. The power and prestige of the babaylan resided in her command of traditional knowledge and capacity to mediate with the spirits to heal, ensure a bountiful harvest or a good catch, or intercede individually or collectively for the good of the community. The babaylan were demonized during the Spanish colonial period and were gradually replaced by an all-male priesthood;[20] the

---

[18] Philippine Preparatory Group, "A Philippine Search for a Liberation Spirituality," in *Asian Christian Spirituality: Reclaiming Traditions*, ed. Virginia Fabella, Peter K.H. Lee, and David Kwang-sun Suh (Maryknoll, NY: Orbis Books, 1992), 101–2.

[19] Fe Mangahas and Jenny R. Llaguno, eds., *Centennial Crossings* (Manila: C&E Publishing, 2006).

[20] Carolyn Brewer, *Holy Confrontation: Religion, Gender and Sexuality in the Philippines, 1521–1685* (Manila: Institute of Women's Studies, St. Scholastica's College, 2001), 183–227.

rights of indigenous women in Philippine lowland society were also taken away. These rights included the right to own properties, to have children regardless of marital status, to retain one's maiden name after marriage, and to initiate and obtain a divorce that is fair to both parties. It is important to note that while male leaders who stood to gain from the new patriarchal religion seem to have more readily capitulated to the Spanish colonizers, it was the babaylan who persisted longer in the resistance.[21] If feminism is defined as the awareness of women's oppression in society and action to transform the situation, then the babaylan are indeed the Philippines' protofeminists and the iconic symbol of female power and leadership in the Philippines.

By the mid-1980s, feminist writings on the babaylan began to proliferate, including Mananzan's *The Filipino Women Before and After the Spanish Conquest of the Philippines.*[22] Feminists began to see themselves as modern babaylan, or as embodying the spirit of the babaylan.[23]

It was only in 2008, however, with the publication of Carolyn Brewer's *Shamanism, Catholicism and Gender Relations in Colonial Philippines, 1521–1685,*[24] that a comprehensive study on the babaylan and their conflict with the Spanish

---

[21] Ibid., 309–50.

[22] Mary John Mananzan, *The Filipino Women Before and After the Spanish Conquest of the Philippines* (Manila: Institute of Women's Studies, St. Scholastica's College, 2003); see also Aida F. Santos, "Do Women Really Hold Up Half the Sky: Notes on Women's Movements in the Philippines," in *Gender, Culture & Society: Selected Readings in Women's Studies in the Philippines*, ed. Carolyn Sobritchea (Seoul: EWHA Womans University Press and Asian Center for Women's Studies, 2004), 23–42; Pennie S. Azarcon, ed., *Kamalayan* (Manila: Pilipina, 1987).

[23] Mary John Mananzan, *The Woman Question in the Philippines* (Manila: Institute of Women's Studies, 1997).

[24] Carolyn Brewer, *Shamanism, Catholicism and Gender Relations in Colonial Philippines, 1521–1685: Women and Gender in the Early Modern World* (Farnham, UK: Ashgate, 2004).

clergy was undertaken. Though the only sources were in Spanish, Brewer used discourse analysis to read these texts from a feminist perspective and to illustrate how Spanish colonizers in the Philippines represented indigenous women and reconstructed gender relations, and also to describe the babaylan resistance to colonization.

Lived Feminist Spiritualities in Subaltern Religious Communities

Fascination with the babaylan led bai theologians to spend time in Mount Banahaw, in search for "living babaylan."[25] Mount Banahaw is a revered spiritual center and a destination for thousands of pilgrims, especially during the Lenten season. It is home to more than eighty homegrown religious movements,[26] a number of which have female priests—such as the Ciudad Mistica de Dios and the Tres Personas Solo Dios (Alliance of Three Persons in One God).

Mount Banahaw has nationalist significance because it was the base of Cofradia de San Jose, a nationalist group in the nineteenth century that fought for religious liberty. Other similar religious-nationalist groups established in the early twentieth century also settled in Banahaw, which was considered by its residents to be the New Jerusalem.[27] Hermano Pule (Apolinario de la Cruz), the leader of Cofradia, had wanted to become a priest but was rejected because he was a native. He then organized the Cofradia as a community of native women and men practicing Christian virtues. It attracted those who were not happy with the rule of the Spaniards and those who wished to go back to the traditional religion. The Spaniards accused the Cofradia of being a political group disguised as

---

[25] Santos, "Do Women Really Hold Up Half the Sky."

[26] Heather L. Claussen, *Unconventional Sisterhood: Feminist Catholic Nuns in the Philippines* (Ann Arbor: University of Michigan Press, 2001).

[27] David C. Lee, "Some Reflections about the Cofradia de San Jose as a Philippine Religious Uprising," *Asian Studies* 9, no. 2 (1971): 126–43.

a religious group and began to persecute them, even as Pule continued to ask for both ecclesial and colonial recognition. Hermano Pule was eventually executed, becoming "the first Filipino martyr to the cause of religious liberty."[28] The founder of Ciudad Mistica, Maria Bernarda Balitaan, had wanted to become a religious sister but, like Pule, was rejected because she is a native; she eventually formed Ciudad Mistica around the turn of the twentieth century. When asked about its mostly female priesthood, the community's current leader, Suprema Isabel, distances their practice from the babaylan tradition. Bai theologian Arche Ligo, in her study "Searching for Babaylan in Ciudad Mistica de Dios," interprets this as a way the group protects itself from charges of paganism and persecution from church and civil authorities.[29] For Mistica, however, the practice is rooted more in the Bible—particularly in the Genesis creation of both man and woman in God's image, implying that there is also a maleness and femaleness in God.

Instead of desperately seeking the babaylan in Mistica and other religious movements today, a fruitful starting point for indigenizing bai theology is to focus on their lived spiritualities as communities of resistance. Even if the female priesthood of Mistica is not traceable to the precolonial babaylan, its existence among the subalterns constitutes a powerful indirect critique of the dominant masculinist Catholic Church hierarchy and structure. Ofelia Villero is right to point out that Mistica does not see itself as a model of resistance to patriarchal institutions.[30] However, although they may have a peaceful coexistence with the parish priest today, the histories of groups in

---

[28] "Who is Hermano Puli?" *Philippine Star*, June 29, 2015.

[29] Arche Ligo, "Searching for Babaylan in Ciudad Mistica de Dios," in *Centennial Crossings*, ed. Fe Mangahas and Jenny R. Llaguno (Manila: C&E Publishing, 2006), 90.

[30] Ofelia O. Villero, "Religion, Gender, and Postcoloniality: the Case of 'Ciudad Mistica de Dios,'" (PhD diss., Graduate Theological Union, Berkeley, California, October 2010).

Mount Banahaw, including Mistica, point to nationalist-religious-gender conflicts that have shaped these religious movements into what they are today.

From a postcolonial reading, Mistica is a hybrid religion—a new cultural form that is neither Christian nor native.[31] Mistica is not Christian: the followers view Maria Bernarda Balitaan, their founder, as bringing to fulfillment the saving work of Jesus, and thus for Mistica, she is the ultimate savior; they retain animist beliefs; they view national hero José Rizal as the Tagalog Christ and the nationalist revolutionaries as saints. It is not orthodox Christian as they have female persons in the Trinity—the Trinity or Sagrada Familia includes God the Father and Mother, the Anak (inclusive Filipino term for son or daughter), and the Holy Spirit (also called by a female title).

However, Mistica is no longer a primal religion; the followers interpret their female priesthood as biblically based. Mistica has appropriated Christian symbols and beliefs, but it has also resisted practices that are inimical to its deeply held traditional belief in the Motherhood of God and women's spiritual leadership.

From the perspective of ethics, Elizabeth Johnson argues that with the globalization of women's advocacy for the equal dignity and rights of women, a change in our God language to include a female image of God that is not seen as a dualism between feminine and masculine characteristics has deep potential of effecting a shift in behavior and religious systems.[32] In Mistica, the Motherhood of Maria Bernard Balitaan is not based on her physical motherhood—it focuses on her being the source of all creation, salvation, and holy wisdom. She and the

---

[31] Agnes M. Brazal, "Female Image of God and Women's Leadership in Ciudad Mistica de Dios," in *Asian Christianities*, ed. Daniel Franklin Pilario, Felix Wilfred, and Huang-Po (London: SCM Press, 2018), *Concilium* 1(2018), 83–92.

[32] Elizabeth Johnson, "Naming God She: The Theological Implications" (2000), Boardman Lectureship in Christian Ethics 5, http://repository.upenn.edu/boardman/5.

Suprema are called "mother" for their status as women leaders "charged with the care of thousands of 'children' with whom they are related in spirit."[33] The integration of this female God language leads the community to a high regard for women and their leadership capacities, posing a challenge to cultural practices within the Catholic Church.

Aside from trekking to Mount Banahaw, bai theologians have started looking for feminist elements in the lived spiritualities of other indigenous groups in the country, their understanding of nature's sacredness, and the link between liberation and creation spiritualities in women's struggle for full humanity.[34] Female priesthood and female images of God in the religious movements in Mount Banahaw and in indigenous groups provide bai theologians with a grounding of feminist ideas in the vernacular culture that is not just a romantic idealization of babaylan history.

Vernacular Categories as Alternative Hermeneutical Lenses

Another approach to postcolonial bai theologizing is the use of vernacular categories to understand—but not necessarily translate—concepts that are foundational for theologizing,

---

[33] Villero, "Religion, Gender, and Postcoloniality," 105.

[34] An example is the study of Felice Imaya Calingayan, OSB, of the Ifugao culture. She herself belongs to a family of Mumbaki, the religious leaders of the Ifugao native religion, a fact that she was ashamed of until her exposure to the Christian indigenous aspect of feminist theologizing and rituals. She describes their God, Kabuniyan, as a community of divine beings, male and female, from different regions, and without a hierarchy. "The words *Kabunyan, kabunhiyan, mabunhiyan,* and *bunhiyan* and the concepts that can be derived from these words suggest a view of the earth as an extension of the Divine. The Divine is in the earth and the earth is in the Divine. After all, the first human beings came from the heavens." "Feminism and Indigenous Spirituality," in *Roots and Routes,* ed. Fabella and Brazal.

such as gender. In the article "Harmonizing Power-Beauty," I explored, in the context of mothers working abroad and the identity crisis of fathers left behind, a more gender-fluid anthropology drawing from a Philippine vernacular construct, *lakas-ganda*.[35]

Lakas refers to physical strength/power but may also be interpreted as inner strength or courage (*lakas ng loob*), and *ganda* can refer to physical beauty but also gracious goodness (*ganda ng loob*).[36] The lakas-ganda construct is deeply embedded in the Philippine psyche. A popular Philippine creation myth tells the story of the first man-woman springing simultaneously from a bamboo. It is conjectured that it was Spanish colonizers in the sixteenth century who named the man Malakas (strong) and the woman Maganda (beautiful), possibly to impose a complementary and dualistic gender ideology. However, this dualism has been subverted in Philippine discourses in which the powerful female or male is someone who exhibits both strength and beauty (whether physical or moral). One finds this in representations of the babaylan, in folk Catholicism, and in the two symbols of female power that emerged in the EDSA revolution—the political activist and the militant nun.

In dialogue with the Christian tradition, I employed the vernacular category of lakas-ganda to reinterpret Sophia and Jesus in terms of power and beauty. God as Sophia in the Book of Wisdom[37] is the female personification of divine power who suffuses the universe and is, at the same time, an image of God's goodness or ganda (Wis 7:29, Prov 8:20). Jesus, as Spirit-Sophia made flesh,[38] showed ganda, gracious goodness,

---

[35] "Harmonizing Power-Beauty: Gender Fluidity in the Migration Context," *AsianChristian Review* 4, no. 2 (Winter 2010): 32–46.

[36] As noted in Chapter 1, *loob* refers to the will or inner self of the person.

[37] Elizabeth Johnson, *She Who Is: Mystery of God in Feminist Theological Discourse* (New York: Crossroad, 1992), 91–92.

[38] Ibid., 94–100.

when he welcomed the children to come to him and when like a mother he fed the hungry multitude. Jesus likewise exhibited lakas, or inner strength, in his fidelity to his commitment to God's reign when he was able to withstand the criticisms of the Pharisees and the taunting of the soldiers while hanging on the cross.

This combination of strength and beauty is a quality that wives and husbands can nurture as they negotiate their gender identities in the migration context. The men left behind are strong when they manage well the wife's earnings and when they are able to withstand ridicule and criticisms by their in-laws and communities for doing work traditionally done by mothers. The women who migrate manifest strength in their hopeful risk-taking, despite what awaits them in the host country, when they endure the loneliness of physical separation from their loved ones, and in their steadfast fidelity to their commitment to the welfare of their families. They exhibit ganda (gracious goodness) as they try to continue to be mothers to their children and show their affection for them even from afar.[39]

The use of vernacular categories (such as lakas-ganda) as hermeneutical lenses allows bai theologians not only to intelligibly communicate the faith to Filipinos in response to concrete contexts but also to offer the Christian community an alternative worldview for articulating Christian faith and practice.

Narrative Theology

Bai theologizing employs narrative theology. By this, I refer to the focus on stories to elucidate Christian teachings. Storytelling has been used widely by feminist theologians, as stories

---

[39] The lakas-ganda understanding of gender differs from the dualistic notion of masculine and feminine in Pope John Paul II's writings. It is also distinct from the perspective of the masculine and feminine in the work of Popes Benedict XVI and Francis, which holds the following: (1) masculine is linked to manhood and feminine to womanhood; (2) the ideal is not in the harmonious unity of masculine and feminine in a person.

speak not only at the cognitive but also the affective level. They can reflect to us who we are and allow us to enter new worlds and be transformed by them. There are many ways in which biblical stories are expressed narratively in the Philippine context, such as the *panunuluyan*—the popular reenactment during Advent of Mary and Joseph's search for a dwelling just before Jesus's birth. There is also the *pasyon*, which is a nonstop chanting of salvation history with a focus on Jesus's passion and death, as well as the *senakulo*, a passion play common in the countryside during Holy Week.

Informed by a Philippine liberationist perspective, bai theologians foreground the voices of marginalized biblical and contemporary women.[40] The narrative approach in particular has been useful to them in showing the relevance of the Bible to women today. As Andrew McKie pointed out in his study of Paul Ricoeur on narrative and ethics, stories can either confess ethics or confound ethics. There are narratives that help toward "an understanding of the good life," and other narratives that might hide or obscure "the Good." In the latter case "the Good is to be perceived by its 'lack,' rather than its presence."[41]

Although acknowledging differences in contexts, bai theologians point to parallels in the stories of marginalized women in the Bible and in stories and situations of today's women in the majority world, both in their exploitation and in their resistance to oppression. Some stories, like that of Judette Gallares's reading of Ruth and Naomi, "confess ethics" in their

---

[40] Judette A. Gallares, *Images of Faith: Spirituality of Women in the Old Testament from a Third World Perspective* (Metro-Manila: Cenacle Philippines and Claretian Publications, 1992), 1–8.

[41] Andrew McKie, "Narrative and Ethics in the Literary Hermeneutics of Paul Ricoeur: An Exploration within the Context of Professional Health Care Education," in *Confessions: Confounding Narrative and Ethics*, ed. Eleanor Milligan and Emma Woodley (Cambridge: Cambridge Scholars Press, 2010), 161–80.

companionship in life transitions.[42] The story of the unnamed concubine of a Levite who was thrown out to be raped in place of the Levite himself and was dismembered by the latter simply "confounds ethics"—according to Helen Graham, in her response to the narrative-interviews of fourteen Filipinas who were sexually violated. As Graham noted, the value of this narrative can be understood only when seen in the context of Israel's descent into chaos, leading to its destruction and exile. And although 2,500 years separate the stories of the fourteen Filipina women and the biblical women, "there is a shocking timelessness about the violence that is narrated."[43]

Bibliodrama as a way of interpreting scripture texts has also been endorsed by the Philippine Episcopal Commission for Biblical Apostolate. Bai theologians have used it for interpreting texts from a feminist perspective in a pastoral context. Bibliodrama is a form of midrash that allows interpreters to give voice to biblical women who are silent, to ask new questions, and to offer new answers. Midrash, a method of interpretation used in rabbinic commentaries on the Hebrew Bible, allows for expansions of the narrative to respond to the questions of the reading community. For example, Ruth's exclamation, "Your God will be my God," is filled out through midrash, such as by having Naomi teach Ruth to observe the Sabbath and not to travel beyond set boundaries on the Sabbath day.

The simplest form of bibliodrama asks participants to sit in a circle. The biblical story is read line by line, and the facilitator asks about "facts" or about elicited emotions. For example, in the story of Cain and Abel, when Cain's offering is rejected, the group can be asked, "Cain, how do you feel now toward your brother?" Anybody in the group can respond. Questions

---

[42] Gallares, *Images of Faith*, 89–126.

[43] Helen Graham, "Victim-Survivors of Sexual Violence in Biblical Perspective," paper presented at the DAKATEO Annual Conference, "Sexual Violence against Women," Tagaytay City, October 24–25, 2008.

can also be asked to absent voices such as Cain's wife or Abraham's mother, or even to animals or objects. It therefore facilitates the foregrounding of silenced voices and of resistance as advocated in postcolonial feminist interpretations. Peter Pitzele, who developed bibliodrama, says that when we get overwhelmed by the various interpretations, we can always return to the written text for the exact word or phrase from which we began.[44] In addition, the feminist hermeneutical principles formulated by bai theologians in 1990 can still be critically appropriated today for narrative theology and biblical interpretations (including bibliodrama) that require some closure. Texts and/or their interpretations are discerned "in accordance with God's design when they promote the [full] humanity of women [and men], foster inclusive communities based on just relations, contribute toward national sovereignty and autonomy, and develop caring and respectful attitudes not only among human beings but toward the rest of creation."[45]

Reading "Close to the Ground"

Bai theologizing is grounded in local concerns and cultural sensitivities and selectively chooses what to appropriate from feminism abroad.

For instance, as in other countries in Asia, bai theologians didn't begin to focus on the issue of sexuality until the 1990s. This is because of the strong cultural taboo in discussing matters of sexuality, which were regarded as private issues. And although the US American second-wave feminism put orgasm, masturbation, and the clitoris into public discourse, this would be unimaginable within Asian cultures. Sexuality issues raised

---

[44] Peter Pitzele, *Scripture Windows: Toward a Practice of Bibliodrama* (Los Angeles: Torah Aura Productions, Alef Design Group, 1998).

[45] Rosario Batung, RGS, Virginia Fabella, Arche Ligo, Mary John Mananzan, and Elizabeth Tapia, "Toward an Asian Principle of Interpretation: A Filipino Woman's Experience," in *Theology/Spirituality of Struggle Series 1991 Series A7* (Manila: FIDES, IWS and EATWOT, 1991), 18.

in the mid-1990s instead focused on prostitution and sexual violence against women.[46] Bai theologians brought to the fore militarized prostitution in the context of the US military bases, comfort women, sex tourism, and trafficking. With Manila having gained a reputation as a sex capital in Asia, along with Bangkok, bai theologians have also focused on deconstructing the Orientalist narrative of Filipinas as exotic, erotic, and submissive women. The issue of artificial contraception has also been approached, not from the standpoint of women's right to sexual pleasure but in the context of the good of the family (e.g., quality of life, husband-wife relationship, population, and available resources).

Another example would be writings related to cybertechnologies whose expanded use in the country has created a new culture that needs to be interrogated from a feminist perspective. Bai theologians wrote about call centers, global capitalism and women, masculinist representations of Filipinas on the internet, the digital divide, how migrants employ cybertechnologies for better or for worse, and cyberchurch of migrants in the Middle East where worship in public places is prohibited or inaccessible.[47]

Alliance with Pro-Feminist Men

Transcending the binary construction of men as oppressors and women as oppressed, bai theologians welcome the collaboration of men as allies of feminist advocacies. Bai

---

[46] See Mary John Mananzan, "Prostitution in the Philippines," in *Challenges to the Inner Room: Selected Essays and Speeches on Women* (Manila: Institute of Women's Studies, St. Scholastica's College, 1998), 196–208; "Theological Reflections on Violence against Women," *Voices* 17, no. 1 (June 1994): 58–69; Mary John Mananzan et al., ed., *Women Resisting Violence: Spirituality of Life* (Maryknoll, NY: Orbis Books, 1996).

[47] See essays in Agnes M. Brazal and Kochurani Abraham, *Feminist Cyberethics in Asia: Religious Discourses on Human Connectivity* (New York: Palgrave Macmillan, 2014).

theologians have benefited from the support of pro-feminist men in the church.

In 1992, the Women and Gender Commission initially formed to raise consciousness of women religious about issues affecting women, was also accepted as a working arm of the Association of Major Religious Superiors in the Philippines. Its goal has been expanded to promote Christian feminism. It mentions among its rationale that "women-men partnership enriches the Church with a unique giftedness. . . . Based on equality as children of God and mutuality as persons, partnership makes for a creative, co-responsible, cooperative concern for the whole Church . . . and a holistic life on planet Earth."[48]

Through the help of supportive males, women theologians also gained entry into major theological schools for ordained ministry, so that they could eventually teach feminist theology subjects and/or integrate feminist concerns into foundational courses. Special acknowledgment should be given to the Scheut Fathers of the Maryhill School of Theology (part of the CICM),[49] the first to open its doors for the theological education of laypeople and the first school for ordained ministry to have a female dean (in the 1990s). At one point in its history, 40 percent of its faculty members were women.

Pro-feminist male theologians integrate feminist concerns in their courses and also write on issues from a feminist perspective.[50] More recently, they lent support toward a more nuanced debate on the reproductive health bill that eventually was passed into law.[51]

---

[48] Leonila Bermisa, MM, "The Women and Gender Commission and the Emergence of Feminist Consciousness among Women Religious," in *Roots and Routes*, ed. Fabella and Brazal.

[49] The CICM Missionaries in the Philippines: *Congregatio Immaculati Cordis Mariae.*

[50] They include Lode Wostyn, CICM, Percy Bacani, MJ, Emmanuel S. de Guzman, Dennis Gonzalez, Daniel Franklin Pilario, and Aloysius Cartagenas.

[51] See, for example, Eric Genilo, "The Catholic Church and the

Reception of Bai Theology

We have so far elaborated five key characteristics of bai theologizing: (1) the shift from nationalist to postcolonial feminism; (2) reconstruction of feminist vernacular elements; (3) employment of narrative theology; (4) reading "close to the ground"; and (5) alliance with pro-feminist men. How has bai theology been received by other women religious and by colleges, theological schools, and the church hierarchy in its three decades of development?

Women Religious

The initial impact of bai theology was strongest among women religious. We have already noted the formation of the Women and Gender Commission (WGC) to raise consciousness of women religious about issues affecting women, including prostitution and US military bases, sex tours, human trafficking, violence against women, and women's status in the church.[52]

Since 1997, with interest in vernacular liturgies growing, the WGC has been advancing the practice of indigenizing liturgies by incorporating the babaylan as special ancestors of Philippine women. It has also been training women religious in feminist interpretation of the Bible and in 2001 started a "Pastoral Ministry toward Healing of Sexually Abused Women." One religious congregation allowed its old residence to house women victim survivors of clergy sexual abuse. This center was named Talitha Cum.[53]

Reproductive Health Bill Debate: The Philippine Experience," *Heythrop* 55 (2014): 1044–55.

[52] Bermisa, "The Women and Gender Commission."

[53] A reference to a story in Mark's Gospel in which Jesus is summoned by the anguished family of a little girl who has just died. Jesus says to them, "'Why all this commotion and wailing? The child is not dead but asleep.' But they laughed at him" (Mk 5:39–40). After sending everyone else out of the room, "He took her by the hand and said to her, '*Talitha*

Women's Colleges and Adult Education

Two colleges in the Philippines have significantly promoted women's studies: Miriam College, formerly owned by the Maryknoll missionaries, and St. Scholastica's College, run by Benedictine Sisters. Miriam College established a Women and Gender Institute in 2000,[54] and St. Scholastica's College founded the Institute of Women's Studies in 1985. Together with Assumption College, which is managed by the Religious of the Assumption, they organized a consortium of women's colleges geared toward the formation of women leaders who will work for women's empowerment and social transformation.

In particular, the Institute of Women's Studies at St. Scholastica's College has an intercultural program whose main achievement is "the training of hundreds of feminist leaders across Asia who are replicating the feminist training that they received from the Institute."[55] As an introduction to gender issues, participants in their trainers' training program make a pilgrimage to Mount Banahaw.[56] The institute also has a "Women and Ecology Wholeness Farm," which demonstrates an alternative lifestyle that is environment-friendly, junk-free, and sustainable. It practices organic, biodiverse farming, and biogas-based waste management. Along a similar line, the Maryknoll Sisters at Miriam College have an Ecological Sanctuary.

On the level of basic ecclesial communities (BECs), the impact of bai theology is hardly felt except in BECs managed by women religious with a feminist orientation. In 2001,

---

cum!' (which means 'Little girl, I say to you, get up!'). Immediately the girl stood up and began to walk around (she was twelve years old). At this they were completely astonished" (Mk 5:41–43).

[54] The Women and Gender Institute continued and built upon the work of the college's Women's Resource and Research Center, which was started in 1987.

[55] Sobritchea, "Country Report on the Philippines," 102–3.

[56] Interview with Merian Aldea, Training Coordinator at the Institute for Women's Studies, 2017.

the Institute of Missiology (Aachen, Germany) conducted an international survey of small Christian communities on "Gender and Church: The Role of the Women."[57] Based on survey results from interviews of women members conducted in five BECs from various parts of the Philippines, the following are the most important women's issues: poverty and joblessness (listed by 44 percent of respondents), violence in the form of wife battery/verbal abuse (28 percent), sexual harassment/abuse (28 percent), women's health (28 percent), marital conflicts/extramarital affairs/vices of men and women (26 percent), gender discrimination/male domination (24 percent), and reproductive issues (use of contraception/abortion) (18 percent). Although 92 percent articulated that it is possible to talk about problems facing women such as violence, male/husband domination, women's health, and sexual abuse in the community, only 28 percent explicitly expressed that they can do this within the BECs.

In four of the five BECs, it was expressed in various parts of the interview that there is little to no discussion within the BECs on gender issues, women's health issues, wife battery, child molestation, and family problems. There is an urgent need for consciousness-raising on these issues—some people, for example, are not even aware that what they are experiencing is molestation.

Theological Institutions

Bai theologian Niceta Vargas, OSA, studied the impact of feminist theologizing on five Catholic schools of theology in Metro-Manila from 1990 to 2011. Her study revealed that in that period, a total of seventy-nine MA/PhD theses on feminist issues were defended and fifty-six articles published in the theological schools' journals. The feminist orientation has been institutionalized at Quezon City's Institute of Formation in

---

[57] I was the coordinator of the research in the Philippines.

Religious Studies, which focuses on the formation of women religious. Directed by bai theologians, it has integrated women's concerns into its mission. It has also been offering an MA religious studies program, and a major in women and religion that began as an MA in feminist theology in 1994.

In other theological schools there is a lack of clear concern about feminist/women's issues in the articulation of their visions, missions, and goals. This generally leads to the marginalization of these issues in the school curriculum, except when bai theologians handle core courses where they are able to integrate feminist perspectives even when this is not explicitly articulated as a thrust of the institution. This integration was the case at the Maryhill School of Theology from the mid-1990s to 2011, resulting in feminist academic production in terms of theses and publications in numbers comparable to those emerging from the Institute of Formation in Religious Studies. In some schools, feminist theology and closely related subjects are in the list of possible course offerings for a degree. Whether these are actually offered or not is largely dependent on the presence of a handful of feminist professors who can be tapped to teach these subjects.

As for the seminarians, a 2004 survey of Philippine seminaries shows that although seminarians no longer believe in the natural inequality of women and men, "almost half of respondents (44.8 percent) are undecided or gave no response when asked to describe their relations with females who are involved in their training." They are likewise "undecided" or "gave no response" when queried about the equality of men and women in assuming leadership positions in church organizations. They ranked women and gender issues as among the least of their concerns. It is not clear to what extent this attitude of seminarians has changed in the past decade.[58]

---

[58] Episcopal Commission on Seminary Formation and the Office on Women of the Catholic Bishops Conference of the Philippines (CBCP), *Benchmark Survey of Philippine Seminaries 2004, Profiles of Theology*

Church Hierarchy

The release of a Protocol on Clergy Sexual Misconduct may be the most important contribution to date of bai theology to the church hierarchy. In 2000, the Women and Gender Commission led by bai theologian Leonila Bermisa, MM, sent a "Proposed Content for a Pastoral Letter on Women"[59] to a conference of Philippine bishops held in 2001. It elaborated on various cases of violence against women, including that of clergy sexual abuse. The inclusion of the latter did not please some bishops who dismiss this issue as "isolated cases" that have been unduly amplified by the influence of feminists trained abroad. After dialogues with the Episcopal Commission for Mutual Relation between Religious and Bishops (ECMR), the bishops, still unsatisfied, asked the Women and Gender Commission to prove its claims. In 2001, its research team started documenting cases. After six months, they had documented thirty cases, plus eleven phone and text messages from victims.[60] The "media managed to get hold of parts" of the report and published it in the "country's most widely read newspaper."[61] This encouraged other women's groups to begin coming out with their own information about clergy sexual misconduct,[62] an issue the bishops could no longer ignore.

It is not difficult to deduce, based on Bermisa's narration in her book, *That She May Dance Again*, that the results of the

---

Seminarians: Values and Relationships vis-à-vis Women's Perspectives and Ecclesial Concerns.

[59] See Appendix A in Nila Bermisa, MM, *That She May Dance Again: Rising from Pain of Violence against Women in the Philippine Catholic Church* (Quezon City: WGC-AMRSP, 2011), 139–44.

[60] Ibid., 72–73.

[61] Bermisa, "The Women and Gender Commission."

[62] Ibid. In response to the increasing number of cases, Bermisa created and supervised (from 2003 to 2005) Talitha Cum, a healing center for the victim-survivors of clergy sexual abuse. The center provided temporary shelter and medical and professional assistance, and helped set up meetings with the superiors of alleged perpetrators.

research started in 2000 had a direct influence on the publication of the 2003 Protocol on Clergy Sexual Misconduct by the Catholic Bishops Conference of the Philippines, the first document of its kind released in the majority world. It is not a perfect document, of course.[63] Its limitations include the following: (1) it did not establish a body to monitor its implementation; (2) it failed to link patriarchal gender socialization patterns and clericalism to sexual violence against women; (3) it does not see the church's hierarchical structure as a factor in the silencing of victims; and (4) unlike other local churches, it does not have a comprehensive plan to respond to cases of sexual abuse.[64] The 2003 document was revised/updated by the CBCP in 2012, but this is still awaiting approval from Rome.[65]

Bai theologizing in the Philippines emerged as a theological reflection on the struggles of women against authoritarianism, neocolonialism, neoliberal capitalism, gender, and other forms of domination. It has been shaped very strongly by the need to define itself as homegrown, in response to accusations that bai theologians are simply imitating Western feminism. The bai response took the form of a strong indigenizing orientation that characterized the articulation of bai feminism since the post-1980s. These theologians would reconstruct vernacular feminist elements and seek to "read the situation 'on the

---

[63] Aloysius Cartagenas, "The Terror of the Sexual Abuse by the Roman Catholic Clergy and the Philippine Context," *Asian Horizons* 5, no. 2 (June 2011): 348–71.

[64] See Canadian Bishops' Committee, "Fifty Recommendations: The Church and Child Sexual Abuse," *Origins* 22, no. 7 (June 25, 1992): 97–107 and US Conference of Catholic Bishops, "When I Call for Help: A Pastoral Response to Domestic Violence against Women," *Origins* 32, no. 24 (November 21, 2002): 399–403.

[65] Paterno Esmaquel II, "What Do Church Rules Say about Ex-Jesuit's Sex Abuse Case?" https://www.rappler.com/newsbreak/in-depth/113963-jesuit-sex-abuse-church-cbcp-rules.

ground,'" gathering selected elements in feminist ideas from abroad that they would adapt. Staying close to Filipinos' love for storytelling, bai theologizing also oftentimes employs narratives for theologizing. It maximizes the use of stories, particularly scripture stories, to foreground women's exploitation and resistance. Last, bai theologies ally with pro-feminist men to bring about changes in attitudes and structures, particularly in male-dominated church institutions.

The growth of bai theologizing is undeniable. It has been aided not only by local organizations but also by transnational networks or associations that make possible the exchange of ideas, publications, and across-the-border organizing. Bai theologians are well-connected internationally through the EATWOT, the EWA, and the nuns with their religious congregations. The reception of bai theologizing is most positive in institutions led by women religious and where alliances of bai professors/women religious with pro-feminist men are strongest. Even as they are situated in the margins of the church hierarchy, these connections and alliances have allowed them to exert some influence and to form the next generation of feminists.

In the future, bai theologizing needs to engage more in dialogue with Muslim feminists, continue its ecofeminist thrust with special focus on the issue of climate change and related disasters, and address LGBTQ issues that theologians continue to evade even as Filipino social scientists have already started probing into these formerly taboo issues.

CHAPTER FOUR

Ecological Cultural Struggles of Indigenous Peoples:
Toward Sustainability as Flourishing

In 2015, Victoria Tauli Corpuz, UN Special Rapporteur on the Rights of Indigenous People in the Philippines, reported that in the last three years, an estimated 100 indigenous persons (hereafter, IPs) were assassinated for securing their homes and ecological milieu.[1] In the name of development, IPs have been subjected to arrests and extrajudicial killings as they try to protect their claim over the land and natural resources. The indigenous groups of the Philippines constitute approximately 12 to 15 million people, making up 10 to 15 percent of the Philippine population, and totaling between 70 and 140 ethnic groups.[2] Most of them (61 percent) reside in Mindanao, in the southern part of the Philippines, and the rest are concentrated in the Cordilleras, in the northern part of the Philippines.

---

[1] "Philippines: 100 Indigenous Peoples Protecting Environment Killed in Last 3 Years—UN Special Rapporteur," Indigenous Voices in Asia, 2015. In 2018, Corpuz was labeled a "terrorist" by President Rodrigo Duterte, http://www.piplinks.org/un-special-rapporteur:-100-indigenous-peoples-protecting-environment-killed-last-3-years.html.

[2] Jacqueline K. Cariño, "Country Technical Note on Indigenous Peoples" (2012), 1, 4, https://www.ifad.org/documents/10180/0c348367-f9e9-42ec-89e9-3ddbea5a14ac.

The UN approach to identifying who is "indigenous" is based on the following: self-identification of an individual and validated by the community; historico-cultural link with precolonial societies; attachment to a land and its natural resources; distinctive culture as compared to the dominant social groups; and intent to preserve their ancestral land and culture as an ethnic group. In the local definition, it is further specified that IPs include their descendants who have retained their distinctive culture but have been displaced from their ancestral land or resettled in other places.[3]

In the Philippines, the indigenous groups consist of tribes who were not strongly influenced by Islamization and by Spanish and US American colonization, mainly due to their resistance to colonization and the inaccessibility of the mountains where most of them resided. This chapter explores their ecological-cultural struggles and how the local churches have been actively engaged in solidarity with their aspirations toward sustainability as flourishing.

Land Conflicts and the Clash of Worldviews

The problem of indigenous peoples in general often revolves around land disputes, as dominant and powerful people use state institutions (police, courts, and military) and laws to gain control of their land and resources.[4] Private parties also use armed groups to grab the lands and gain access to minerals, timber, and other resources. At other times, non-state, armed ideological groups such as the New People's Army—the armed wing of the Communist Party of the Philippines—occupy the

---

[3] Republic Act 8371, "Indigenous People's Rights Act," 1997, http://www.officialgazette.gov.ph/1997/10/29/republic-act-no-8371/; henceforth IPRA.

[4] Victoria Tauli-Corpuz, "Conflict, Peace, and the Human Rights of Indigenous Peoples," presentation given at Columbia University, New York (May 2017), http://unsr.vtaulicorpuz.org/site/index.php/statements/134-conflict-peace-indigenous-rights.

land of IPs and recruit them into their armed struggle. Since they are far from the protection of state institutions, the New People's Army has gained a foothold in those areas. State armed forces, who label and target indigenous peoples as supportive of the communist rebels, harass, threaten, sexually violate, and detain the former. On a deeper level, the conflict on land is also about worldviews.

Indigenous Peoples' View of the Land and Ecology

Indigenous peoples of the Philippines generally believe that land has been granted and entrusted by the Creator for everyone to harness, cultivate, sustain, and live on. This land concept has been expressed in a collectivism that rejects the idea of private ownership of land;[5] there is only the right of use (or usufruct) by individuals that is inseparable from communal use. Although there exist today various forms of land ownership ranging from communal to semicommunal to private, customary laws of the community that continue to evolve normally govern land ownership and control of resources.[6]

Many IPs view the land as sacred and as a collective inheritance that they must protect, especially as they face the threat of losing control over their homeland. In a dialogue between church workers and fourteen indigenous groups from Mindanao in 1977,[7] the IPs upheld the following views:

---

[5] Jose Mencio Molintas, "The Philippine Indigenous Peoples' Struggle for Land and Life: Challenging Legal Texts," *Arizona Journal of International and Comparative Law* 21, no. 1 (2004): 269–306.

[6] Cariño, "Country Technical Note on Indigenous Peoples," 7.

[7] This group includes the following: Subanon, Mamanwa, Bukidnon, Higaonon, Mansaka, Mandaya, Ata, Dibabawon, B'laan, Manobo, Bagobo, T'bolis, Ubo, and Tiruray. See Karl Gaspar, CSsR, *The Lumad's Struggle in the Face of Globalization* (Davao: Ateneo Forum for Research in Mindanao, 2000), 107.

1. As subsistence economies, their major sources of livelihood are the land and its natural resources. Land is God's gift . . . it is a source of life and it is the source of everything they need.
2. The soil is sacred; thus, they pray to it. They believe they came from the soil and to it they will return when they die. The land is where their ancestors are buried, thus further strengthening their link to the land.
3. They believe that God owns the land or that the "land is both a father and a mother."[8] Humans can only develop and sell the fruits of the land but not the land itself.

In the northern part of the Philippines, as can be gleaned in the Kalinga land law from 1983, the land and all the resources including the bodies of water are believed to be owned by the Supreme God, Apo Kabuniyan.[9] The Kalingas are just caretakers of these sacred lands, which are communally owned in a subsistence economy (a nonmonetary economy that relies on natural resources to supply basic needs).

For those engaged in swidden farming (a shifting or rotating form of cultivation), priority is given to the person who has cleared the land and sustained it through constant usage. The Kalingas also have individual private ownership of residential lots and terraced rice farms—this ownership is limited to the parent and their children, including those yet to be born. Any person who disposes of land through sale or exchange faces ostracism. There are occasionally, however, valid grounds for disposing of land, such as grave illness in the family, but only on the condition that the sale is negotiated with a member of the clan, or, at the minimum, with a member of the community.

---

[8] Ibid.

[9] Maria Lourdes Aranal-Sereno and Roan Libarios, "The Interface between National Land Law and Kalinga Land Law," *Philippine Law Journal* 58 (1983): 420.

Clash with Colonizer and
Capitalist Views of the Land and Ecology

The indigenous peoples' view of the land clashes with colonizers' and capitalists' views. The Spanish colonizers introduced the Regalian Doctrine that states that on account of conquest, all the lands belong to the king of Spain. Everyone should thus obtain deeds from the government. The US American colonizers carried out a similar policy. They declared all lands subject to the Torrens system,[10] whereby the state is the official keeper of land titles. The Public Land Act of 1905 prescribed that all lands that were not registered were thereby considered public lands, and that only the State had the right to exploit them. Through this and the Mining Law of 1905, the US Americans were able to access public land for mining purposes.[11]

With Philippine independence, the same system was maintained such that a national written law existed simultaneously with unwritten tribal laws. There was no way to revert ownership once the land was registered under the Torrens system. This facilitated the conversion of the view of land ownership from communal to individual.[12]

Since the 1970s, indigenous communities have felt pressure from an economy that has become increasingly export-oriented and foreign-dominated.[13] In the 1980s, the International Monetary Fund, through its structural adjustment program for heavily indebted nations like the Philippines, pushed for liberalization, deregulation, and cheaper tariffs for goods. This

---

[10] A system of land title registration invented by Sir Robert Torrens of Australia in the mid-nineteenth century.

[11] Molintas, "The Philippine Indigenous Peoples' Struggle for Land and Life."

[12] Aranal-Sereno and Libarios, "The Interface between National Land Law and Kalinga Land Law," 434.

[13] Molintas, "The Philippine Indigenous Peoples' Struggle for Land and Life."

led to even greater exposure of indigenous peoples' lands to mining extraction, logging, chemical-intensive monoculture agricultural plantations, hydro projects, and other environmentally destructive, "renewable" energy projects.[14]

Indigenous Peoples' Rights Act (IPRA)

A positive development in the Philippines resulting from the struggles of IPs is the Indigenous Peoples' Rights Act (IPRA), which became a law in 1997. The Philippines was the first country in Asia to pass a law governing indigenous peoples' rights.[15] The IPRA recognizes the rights of indigenous peoples to hold land titles and to employ their own processes of conflict resolution, promotion of peace, and the granting of justice.

The issuance of the Certificates of Ancestral Domain Claims (CADCs) gives IPs collective rights to a specifically delineated geographic space. Ancestral lands refer to all types of lands and bodies of water continuously occupied or used by IP individuals, families, and clans (except when they were displaced because of government projects or deals with private individuals or corporations, war, deceit, etc.).[16]

IPRA assumes that when people are given the right to manage the land and its resources, they will be more committed to its protection in the long term. This is not, however,

---

[14] Kalipunan ng mga Katutubong Mamamayan ng Pilipinas (KAMP)—National Alliance of Indigenous Peoples Organizations in the Philippines, "Indigenous Peoples: Resist Neoliberal Globalization and Assert Our Right to Self-Determination," 2013, http://iva.aippnet.org/indigenous-peoples-resist-neoliberal-globalization-and-assert-our-right-to-self-determination/.

[15] For laws on land rights of indigenous peoples in Southeast Asia, see Alexandra Xanthaki, "Land Rights of Indigenous Peoples in South-East Asia," *Melbourne Journal of International Law 5*, 2003, http://www5.austlii.edu.au/au/journals/MelbJIL/2003/5.html#Heading46.

[16] IPRA, chap. 2, sec. 3 (b).

necessarily the case,[17] due either to the presence or absence of two crucial factors. First, there should exist transparent and accountable means of decision making on the management of resources. Before any project is begun within ancestral lands, the indigenous people must grant their Free, Prior, and Informed Consent (FPIC). In the past, IPs were often excluded from the planning of development projects that would affect them heavily, such as mining and logging.[18] The requirement for FPIC is meant to address this problem—but intimidation, misinformation, bribery, and tactics of dividing the leaders and the community, are usually employed to obtain the indigenous peoples' consent or to "bulldoze" them into endorsing the project. For instance, one community in Upper Pulangi endorsed a mining exploration "in exchange for Php 5,000 [equivalent to $100] monthly allowance for each of the 20 tribal leaders, 40 college scholarships, and 50 high school scholarships."[19] This tactic contributes to and reinforces the corruption of leaders. It is important that negotiations between the community leaders and the corporations and government agencies are fully transparent.

Indigenous peoples' organizations have also noted that the government-sponsored National Commission on Indigenous Peoples (NCIP) takes the side of mining companies, instead of protecting the rights of IPs, when there are conflicts in the interpretation of laws.[20]

---

[17] June Prill-Brett, "Contested Domains: The Indigenous Peoples Rights Act (IPRA) and Legal Pluralism in the Northern Philippines," *Journal of Legal Pluralism and Unofficial Law* 39, no. 55 (2007): 11–36.

[18] Reynaldo D. Raluto, *Poverty and Ecology at the Crossroads: Towards an Ecological Theology of Liberation in the Philippine Context* (Metro-Manila: Ateneo de Manila University Press, 2015), 23.

[19] Sango Mahanty, "Peter Walpole on Mining and Indigenous Peoples in the Philippines—Interview [1]," Environmental Science for Social Change (ESSC), 2011, http://essc.org.ph/content/view/568/46/.

[20] C. Doyle, C. Wicks, and F. Nally, "Mining in the Philippines: Concerns and Conflicts," Report of a Fact-Finding Trip to the Philippines (West

Only the more organized Cordillera Administrative Region in northern Philippines and the Autonomous Region in Muslim Mindanao in southern Philippines have been strong enough to fight for their rights. As residents of autonomous regions, they have political rights and representation and thus have a much stronger voice compared with other IPs in the country. Second, IPs will be more committed to protecting the resources in their ancestral land if they continue to be convinced that their survival is dependent on their link to the land.[21]

Self-Determination and Cultural Survival

The inability of the land to provide for the basic needs of the IPs is eroding their view of the land as a source of cultural identity and survival. More and more IPs prefer to go to the cities to work, as the land is no longer fertile (possibly due in part to the effects of mining and deforestation).

Kankana-ey farmers who are now into commercial vegetable farming in Benguet unanimously expressed in a 1992 interview with the Department of Environment and Natural Resources that they now prefer individual titles over ancestral land and domain certificates. This is because of their fear that outsiders do not respect their customary tribal laws and that they are more vulnerable to land-grabbing if the land is not individually registered and titled. In another study, Ibaloi elders said that although they prefer customary laws whose rules are more equitable, 90 percent feel there is more protection in an individual title, as land-grabbing has been the experience of those without such titles.[22] In their culture, there is a fear of supernatural sanctions if one grabs the property of another, but lowlanders are less deterred by this.[23]

Midlands, UK: Columban Fathers, 2007), iv, http://www.piplinks.org/system/files/Mining+in+the+Philippines+-+Concerns+and+Conflicts.pdf.

[21] Prill-Brett, "Contested Domains."

[22] Ibid., 30.

[23] See also Nestor Castro, "Three Years of the Indigenous Peoples

The above cases show that some groups of IPs are in danger of losing their lands and will disappear as ethnic groups not because they wish to do so but because they are forced to adopt the system of the lowlanders. It cannot be denied though that there are individuals who aspire to be eventually integrated within the larger Philippine society. In "Cultural Rights: Fribourg Declaration, 2007,"[24] there is neither a stipulation on the duty to preserve one's culture nor a discourse on the right to cultural survival. Among the cultural rights listed in the Fribourg Declaration are respect for cultural identity and the different ways this can be manifested, access to heritages, respect for identification with one or more cultural communities simultaneously regardless of borders, the

---

Rights Act: Its Impact on Indigenous Communities," *Kasarinlan, Philippine Quarterly of Third World Studies* (Special Issue on Indigenous Peoples) 15, no. 2 (2000): 49.

[24] "Cultural Rights: Fribourg Declaration," 2007, http://www1.umn. edu/humanrts/instree/Fribourg%20Declaration.pdf. The declaration presents in one document what have been acknowledged in a number of universal and regional instruments. A skeletal catalogue of what can be considered as cultural rights can already be found in international instruments such as the Universal Declaration of Human Rights (1948) and the International Covenant on Economic, Social and Cultural Rights (ICESCR, 1966), and in regional declarations such as the American Declaration on the Rights and Duties of Men (1948), the Additional Protocol to the American Convention on Human Rights in the Area of Economic, Social and Cultural Rights (1988), and in the African Charter on Human and Peoples' Rights (1981). These documents focus on cultural rights as rights of the individual. The notion of cultural rights as "collective" rights or "group-specific" rights has also been recognized implicitly in the ICESCR and the International Covenant on Civil and Political Rights (ICCPR, 1966); it has been acknowledged explicitly in the 1982 World Conference on Cultural Policies and also in the Declaration on the Rights of Persons Belonging to National or Ethnic, Religious and Linguistic Minorities (1992). A number of other documents cataloging cultural rights have also been produced—see Halina Niec, "Advocating for Cultural Rights: Cultural Rights at the End of the World Decade for Cultural Development," 7, http://kvc.minbuza.nl/uk/archive/commentary/niec.html.

right to identify or not with a particular cultural community, and even the freedom to assume multiple cultural identities. The rights this document lists are also basically rights of the person, which she or he can exercise alone or together with others. Cultural identity in the document is defined as "the sum of all cultural references through which a person, alone or in community with others, defines or constitutes oneself, communicates and wishes to be recognized in one's dignity."[25] Indigenous peoples, as individuals and as communities, have the right to make decisions regarding their identity and cultural survival.

Such a decision is, however, made in the context of a field of power relations, as sociologist Pierre Bourdieu would hold. Bourdieu himself did not speak about cultural rights, but his discourse on [cultural] practice as shaped by *habitus*, *capital*, and *field*, highlights culture as negotiated by individuals in social relation. *Habitus* refers to embodied dispositions or the "cultural unconscious."[26] Bourdieu further notes that, on the one hand, habitus is a "structured structure"; what individuals view as reasonable or unreasonable for people of their status in the social world stems from habitus. In this way habitus perpetuates existing opportunity structures/conditions. On the other hand, habitus is also a "structuring structure"; it has an inventive or creative dimension. The durable dispositions can generate or produce a variety of practices and perceptions in fields beyond those in which the habitus was initially acquired.[27]

---

[25] The declaration defines a cultural community as "a group of persons who share references that constitute a common cultural identity that they intend to preserve and develop." "Cultural Rights: Fribourg Declaration," 2007, Art. 2, 5.

[26] Class distinctions (which, for Bourdieu, include gender, race, ethnicity, place of residence, and age) become embodied in the habitus. Pierre Bourdieu, "What Makes a Social Class? On the Theoretical and Practical Existence of Groups," *Berkeley Journal of Sociology* 32 (1987): 1–17.

[27] Pierre Bourdieu, *Outline of a Theory of Practice*, trans. Richard Nice (Cambridge: Cambridge University Press, 1977; reprint ed. 1998),72.

Capital for Bourdieu can be either economic (what you have—wealth, income, property), social (whom you know—social connections or network), or cultural (what you know—cultivated and embodied dispositions, cultural artifacts, or educational credentials). Their interrelation affects one's position in the field (e.g., the Philippine society or a contested land), which is a site of struggle for the right to speak or the power to legitimate. Cultural practice, Bourdieu emphasized, possesses logic; it is a strategic response in view of one's position in the field of power that maximizes one's economic, cultural, and social capital, or in ordinary lingo, one's well-being.

Backed up by extensive fieldwork, Bourdieu offered in his book *Distinction* the following equation of his general science of cultural practice: [(habitus) (capital) + field] = practice.[28] In Bourdieu's framework, therefore, a cultural right, even when exercised by an individual, is always situated within a community in the form of the role of the following: social structures [field]; the community traditions embedded in one's cultural unconscious [habitus]; and one's position in that field [capital]. IPs who choose to have individual titles are doing so to protect a possible loss of economic capital if the land is considered an ancestral domain, a claim which is more tenuous. Some IPs have very little cultural, economic, and social capital with which they can negotiate with big businesses or resist land-grabbers. They need to be conscientized and organized and given support by the State and by NGOs so they can improve their status and voice in the field of power relations.

Indigenous leaders may also view indigeneity differently. This is apparent in the micropolitics of Sambilog, a people's organization that started out as an indigenous environmental movement in Palawan, Philippines, and whose main advocacy is to regain lost land and fishing rights.[29] Patrik, for example,

---

[28] Pierre Bourdieu, *Distinction: A Social Critique of the Judgment of Taste* (Cambridge, MA: Harvard University Press, 1984), 101.

[29] Noah Theriault, "The Micropolitics of Indigenous Environmental

who had experienced working in Manila, is fighting for land rights not primarily to preserve their culture or protect the environment; it is more about overcoming socioeconomic inequalities. These aims need not be contradictory, of course, but he is more open to being integrated fully into the bigger Philippine society than is his cousin Balong. For Balong, Pala'wan identity is integrally linked to the land. Though married to a non-Pala'wan, he makes a sharper distinction between the indigenous and non-indigenous and stresses that their fight to regain land that was lost is for the natives and not for the settlers from elsewhere.

Noah Theriault pointed out how identity politics based on indigeneity can have advantages and disadvantages. Because of IPRA, indigenous politics can benefit from legal protection; and members of Sambilog focus on the importance of recognizing indigenous rights and aspirations. At the same time, however, individual members are aware that IPs have intersecting concerns with the other marginalized poor in the area. Current membership not only includes indigenous Pala'wan and indigenous Molbog, but also settlers of various ethnicities, and because of this, the issue of "authenticity" has been used against them by their business opponents who accuse them of not being a genuine indigenous group.

A word about ethnic identity is in order here. Identity, as postcolonial theorist Stuart Hall underlined, defines a place or space from which people speak and thus continues to be important. However, identities should no longer be understood in the sense of a unified stable core. Cultural identity is not the "collective or true self hiding inside the many other, more superficial or artificially imposed 'selves' which a people with a shared history and ancestry hold in common and which can stabilize, fix or guarantee an unchanging 'oneness'

---

or cultural belongingness underlying all the other superficial differences."[30]

In relation to this, Hall distinguishes between identity politics and a politics of representation. Identity politics espouses an essentialist notion of identity. A politics of representation, in contrast, goes beyond essentialism and views identity as complexly composed and historically constructed. It moves from either/or binaries to deconstruct the binaries of stereotyping themselves, by focusing on the different forms of representations in their complexities and ambivalences; it is also sensitive to the negative consequences of such positionality for those who are excluded by its discourse. Sambilog is an example of a politics of representation, in which identities remain important but where there is an awareness that being an IP is not only about being indigenous but also about being poor—poverty being a common ground with the non-indigenous poor. Theriault himself endorsed the notion of an indigenous movement such as Sambilog, which is linked to a broader movement for socio-environmental justice and sustainability.

Indigenous Peoples' Sustainability as Flourishing

Indigenous peoples are often blamed for their poverty because they resist the state's neoliberal agenda for economic development. Countering such thinking, the Catholic Bishops Conference of the Philippines (CBCP), in their document *What Is Happening to Our Beautiful Land* (1988), pointed out: "We often use the word progress to describe what has taken place over the past few decades. There is no denying that in some areas our roads have improved and that electricity is more readily available. But can we say that there is real progress? Who has benefitted most and who has borne the real

---

[30] Stuart Hall, "Introduction: Who Needs Identity," in *Questions of Cultural Identity*, ed. Stuart Hall and Paul du Guy (London: Sage, 2000), 4.

costs?" Indeed, this foreign-driven economic model does not promote sustainable development for indigenous peoples; it destroys not only their land and the ecosystem but also weakens their capacity to decide on their future as a people.

Sustainability in the Brundtland Report

Out of concern for social inequality, environmental destruction, and climate change, the Brundtland Commission report, *Our Common Future: Report of the World Commission on Environment and Development*, promoted the concept of sustainable development.[31] It defined sustainability as "development that meets the needs of the present without compromising the ability of future generations to meet their own needs" (no. 27).

The more dominant interpretation of the Brundtland report is that sustainability rests on the three pillars of environmental, social, and economic sustainability, also called the triple bottom-line model. This has often been interpreted as greening, eco-efficiency, and corporate social responsibility within the same economic model that sees economic growth as a measure of progress. This conflation of goals has been abused by mining corporations, for instance, who claim that what they are doing is sustainable and responsible mining.

An alternative interpretation by Erling Holden, Kristin Linnerud, and David Banister identifies four important dimen-

---

[31] The World Commission on Environment and Development, *Our Common Future: Report of the World Commission on Environment and Development* (Oxford: Oxford University Press, 1987). Whereas some scholars would view sustainability as referring only to the environmental aspect of development, or as referring to a process (versus sustainable development, which refers to the product), in this chapter, I am using the terms *sustainability* and *sustainable development* interchangeably. See Erling Holden, Kristin Linnerud, and David Banister, "Sustainable Development: Our Common Future Revisited," *Global Environmental Change* 26 (May 2014): 130–39.

sions of sustainability.[32] First is safeguarding long-term ecological sustainability. Second is satisfying basic needs, especially the needs of the world's poor. The third and fourth dimensions are promoting intragenerational and intergenerational equity both nationally and globally. Note that in contrast to the triple bottom-line model, economic growth is not among the primary dimensions. These scholars pointed out that the Brundtland report stresses that while economic growth is important for lifting people out of poverty, economic growth or living standards that go beyond basic needs can be sustainable only if these can maintain long-term ecological sustainability. This basically limits the growth that developed nations can pursue. Moreover, participation of peoples in decision making is an important aspect of the effort to achieve these four goals. Although this interpretation can prevent the co-optation of "sustainability" by business interests, the perspective of indigenous peoples challenges us to go even further.

Sustaining Flourishing

Sustainability of indigenous peoples as a community is linked to their ancestral land, which nourishes them; the land where their ancestors are buried and where their spirits roam; the land where their spirit guides dwell in the trees, rivers, and mountains; and the land where they, too, will be buried.[33] The ecological destruction of this land is tantamount to their self-destruction as a people.

In line with the IP perspective, John R. Ehrenfeld and Andrew J. Hoffman propose in their book *Flourishing: A Frank Conversation about Sustainability*[34] that to be sustainable further requires a fundamental shift in our way of thinking and

---

[32] Holden, Linnerud, and Banister, "Sustainable Development."

[33] Raluto, *Poverty and Ecology at the Crossroads*, 21.

[34] John R. Ehrenfeld and Andrew J. Hoffman, *Flourishing: A Frank Conversation about Sustainability* (Stanford, CA: Stanford University Press, 2013).

must go to the core of who we are as human beings. It entails a shift from the view of the human as *Homo economicus*—as beings that always use "resources to maximize well-being, happiness, pleasure"[35]—to a view of humans as "being" or living authentically, rather than always "having." To be sustainable is to know who we are and our place in the world.

Ehrenfeld and Hoffman stressed the importance of knowing what we are sustaining and that something is flourishing—the "possibility that humans and other life will flourish on the earth [forever]."[36] Human flourishing is a form of existence based on care. Flourishing results from caring for oneself, other humans, and the rest of the material world, as well as the spiritual or transcendent worlds. For this, Ehrenfeld noted that one must be equipped with certain basic capabilities, as Amartya Sen proposed.

In his book *Development as Freedom*, Sen argued that although increased income is necessary for the poor to gain basic freedoms, beyond this, development or flourishing is no longer dependent on continuous economic growth.[37] Flourishing is measured by the possession of a conglomeration of capabilities that enable people to make choices, which are as follows: (1) economic opportunities; (2) political liberties; (3) social powers such as the enabling conditions of good health and basic education; (4) transparency guarantees (e.g., openness, rights to information, and other evidence of trust); and (5) a sense of safety and security.[38] The main concerns of IPs cited by Filipino anthropologist Karl Gaspar match these basic

---

[35] Ibid., 29.

[36] Ibid., 6. "Forever" refers to the flourishing of the whole system.

[37] Amartya Sen, *Development as Freedom* (New York: Alfred A. Knopf, 2000). See also Deepa Narayan, Robert Chambers, Meera K. Shah, and Patti Petesch, *Voices of the Poor: Crying Out for Change* (New York: Oxford University Press for the World Bank, 2000).

[38] As an example of this, Sen points to how Indians of Kerala outlive African Americans who have higher incomes, illustrating how well-being can be delinked from economic growth.

capabilities listed by Sen: development of their livelihood, self-determination through the exercise of their rights to their ancestral land, an empowering education that nourishes their culture, a healthful ecology, and living peacefully in their communities.[39]

In contrast to Sen though, for Ehrenfeld the freedoms that Sen identified are not ends in themselves but means that allow a person to choose to care (and that thus enable flourishing); Ehrenfeld saw "caring" as an intermediate step to flourishing.[40]

It is interesting to note that many articles about indigenous peoples describe IPs as using the term *flourishing* to refer to their aspirations for their cultures. We recognize, however, that some individual indigenous peoples see leaving their land as the catalyst for their flourishing. Such a decision should, however, be made by individuals equipped with basic capabilities and not simply because they are forced by circumstances or by the very lack of these capabilities.

Sustainability as the creation and maintenance of flourishing should effect a paradigm shift in the way corporations think of their businesses. Their primary role should be to "enable people to flourish—that is, take care of the world around them."[41] Though profit is still important, the basic goal of a corporation should be to contribute to flourishing.

In *Laudato Si'*, Pope Francis also moved beyond the usual understanding of sustainable development by using the phrase "integral and sustainable human development" (nos. 13, 18, 50).[42] As Cardinal Peter Turkson, head of the Pontifical Council for Justice and Peace and one of the key architects of the encyclical, pointed out, this phrase implies more than simply

---

[39] See Karl Gaspar, CSsR, *Panagkutay: Anthropology and Theology Interfacing in Mindanao Uplands (The Lumad Homeland)* (Metro-Manila: Institute of Spirituality in Asia, 2017), xxix.

[40] Ehrenfeld and Hoffman, *Flourishing*, 17.

[41] Ibid.

[42] *Laudato Si'*: On Care for Our Common Home, 2015, http://w2.vatican.va.

adding the word "integral." Integral development, as first laid out in *Populorum Progressio* and reiterated in succeeding church teaching, is the promotion of the good of every person and of the whole person (no. 14). Turkson adds:

> Such multi-faceted development goes well beyond an ever-expanding GDP, even a better-distributed one, and merely economic or material progress. It encompasses the cultural, social, emotional, intellectual, aesthetic, and religious dimensions. It is an invitation for each person on the planet to *flourish*, to use the gifts given to them by God to become who they were meant to be.[43]

Within this "integral and sustainable human development," *Laudato Si'* proposes a reenvisioning of the understanding of humanity's place vis-à-vis the rest of creation, which is also an important aspect in Ehrenfeld's concept of flourishing. The pope employed the metaphor of kinship to speak of creation: "Our common home is like a sister with whom we share our life and a beautiful mother who opens her arms to embrace us" (no. 1). This kin-centric ecology reflects the anthropology of many indigenous peoples. "All of us are linked by unseen bonds and together form a kind of universal family" (no. 89).[44] Like one body, "We can feel the desertification of the soil almost as a physical ailment and the extinction of a species as a painful disfigurement" (no. 89).

Laudato Si' also affirms the "manifestation of God" in creation (no. 85). "The Spirit of life dwells in every living creature" (no. 88). Christ "entered into the created cosmos, throwing in his lot with it, even to the cross" (no. 99). And it is God

---

[43] Cardinal Peter Turkson, "Cardinal Turkson's Address to Global Responsibility 2030," 2016, https://zenit.org/articles/cardinal-turksons-address-to-global-responsibility-2030/. Italics added.

[44] See Chapter 6 for the discussion on creation as gift (*kaloob*), suggesting that we share with creation a common *loob* (inner self).

who ultimately owns creation. As shared inheritance (no. 93), "the world we have received also belongs to those who will follow us" (no. 159).

Strikingly, in describing the role of humans toward creation, the term *care* was used twenty times in *Laudato Si'*, whereas *stewardship* was used only once and that was to qualify what *dominion* means in the Bible. Cardinal Turkson explained this choice of terminology as follows: "Good stewards take responsibility and fulfill their obligations to manage and to render an account. But one can be a good steward without feeling connected. If one cares, however, one is connected. To care is to allow oneself to be affected by another, so much so that one's path and priorities change."[45] As noted earlier, in sustainability as flourishing, it is also through care for one's self and for others that the flourishing of human life and the rest of creation can be brought about. Turkson himself often uses the words *care* and *flourish/flourishing* together.

The Role of the Local Church toward Indigenous Peoples' Flourishing

In the early 1970s, conscientized by the repressive government of Marcos and by liberation theology, many laypeople, sisters, and priests engaged in organizing the poor.[46] This activism on behalf of and with the poor received an additional impetus when some bishops (including Antonio Fortich, Julio Xavier Labayen, OCD, and Francisco Claver, SJ) actively promoted the church of the poor and marginalized in their dioceses despite the repressive conditions prevailing under martial law. Indeed,

---

[45] "Catholics, Capitalism and Climate: Cardinal Turkson Interprets Pope Francis," panel at Molloy College in Rockville Centre, NY, 2016, https://catholicclimatemovement.global/catholics-capitalism-and-climate-cardinal-turkson-interprets-pope-francis/.

[46] Ton Danenberg, Carlos Ronquillo, José M. de Mesa, Emelina Villegas, and Maurice Piers, *Fired from Within: Spirituality in the Social Movement* (Metro-Manila: Institute of Spirituality in Asia, 2007).

in 1973, Bishop Labayen of the Prelature of Infanta challenged the church to "listen to the voice of the many poor."[47]

Seeing that indigenous peoples are among the poorest and most marginalized, in 1977 the Catholic Bishops Conference of the Philippines (CBCP) created the Tribal Filipino Apostolate, a church institution advocating on behalf of indigenous peoples, and designated the second Sunday of every October as Tribal Filipino Sunday.[48] In 1995 this apostolate became the Episcopal Commission on Indigenous Peoples.

In 1991, five years after the first People Power Revolution, the Second Plenary Council of the Philippines (PCP II) approved the vision of the Church as a Community of Christ's Disciples and Church of the Poor. By this, it means (in the words of Pope John XXIII), "A Church of all, but especially of the poor."[49] The characteristics of the Church of the Poor include the following: (1) that it "will collaborate with the poor themselves and with others to lift up the poor from their poverty" (Acts no. 130); (2) that it "will courageously defend and vindicate the rights of the poor and the oppressed, even when doing so will mean alienation or persecution from the rich and powerful" (Acts no. 131); (3) that it is a church where "the poor . . . will participate actively, as equal to others, in her life and mission" (Acts no. 136).[50]

---

[47] Cited by William N. Holden, "From the Church of the Powerful to the Church of the Poor: Liberation Theology and Catholic Praxis in the Philippines," in *The Changing World Religion Map: Sacred Places, Identities, Practices and Politics,* vol. 4, ed. Stanley D. Brunn (Dordrecht: Springer, 2015), 3099.

[48] William N. Holden, "The Least of My Brethren: Mining, Indigenous Peoples, and the Roman Catholic Church in the Philippines," *Worldviews* 17, no. 3 (2013): 211.

[49] From a radio speech of John XXIII in 1962, six weeks before the opening of Vatican II. See also Marcus Mescher, "Fifty Years Later, Are We Still the Church of the Poor?" *Millennial* (2012), http://millennialjournal.com/2012/09/11/fifty-years-later-are-we-still-the-church-of-the-poor/.

[50] Acts and Decrees of the Second Plenary Council of the Philippines (Manila: Catholic Bishops' Conference of the Philippines, 1992).

Though it does not use the liberation theology term *option for the poor*, which some see as more confrontational in approach, the Church of the Poor as described here does not run away from conflict that may be caused by siding with the interest of the poor against the rich and the powerful. PCP II also identified IPs as a sector of society calling for special attention. In particular, it underlined the importance of protecting the cultures, ancestral lands, and the integrity of the environment of the indigenous peoples.[51]

Pastoral Letters on the
Environment and Indigenous Peoples

The church has been very actively engaged with the struggles of indigenous peoples and their opposition to mining, which has replaced illegal logging as the major threat to their survival. To date, the CBCP has issued five pastoral letters and statements that touch on the environment and IPs—in 1988, 1998, 2000, 2006, and 2008. In 1988, alarmed by the rapid deterioration of ecological conditions, the CBCP released the pastoral letter *What Is Happening to Our Beautiful Land?*[52] This is the first pastoral letter by any bishops' conference in the world that is centered solely on ecological issues.[53] The letter noted how "tribal people all over the Philippines, who have seen the destruction of their world at close range, have cried out in anguish."[54] It likewise affirmed the indigenous peoples' worldview and lifestyle,[55] proclaiming: "Our forefathers and our tribal brothers and sisters today still attempt to live in harmony with nature. They see the Divine Spirit in the living

---

[51] Ibid., 130.

[52] CBCP, *What Is Happening to Our Beautiful Land?: A Pastoral Letter on Ecology*, http://www.cbcponline.org/documents/1980s/1988-ecology.html.

[53] Amado Picardal, CSsR, "The Philippine Church's Environmental Advocacy," CBCP News, http://www.cbcpnews.com/cbcpnews/?p=59588.

[54] CBCP, *What Is Happening to Our Beautiful Land?*

[55] Cf. *Laudato Si'*, no. 146.

world and show their respect through prayers and offerings."[56] The pastoral letter also called on the government to support an "ecologically sustainable development."

Pope Francis's encyclical *Laudato Si'*, which cited the CBCP pastoral letter, is an affirmation of the pioneering efforts of the church in the Philippines—including the BECs—to defend the environment over the years. Bishops, priests, and laypeople in various parts of the country have been at the forefront of the struggle against logging, mining, coal-fired power-plant projects, and other anti-environment activities. In 1998, the CBCP issued "A Statement of Concern on the Mining Act of 1995." The Mining Act (passed by the national congress and senate of the Philippines) encourages the exploitation of IP lands by granting mining companies priority access rights to water and timber. Provisions such as these make it easier for the communities to be slowly eased out of their land. The expansion of sites granted with mining permits and clearances eat up considerable portions of land that had been devoted to agriculture. The CBCP statement criticized the fact that "the government mining policy is offering our lands to foreigners with liberal conditions while our people continue to grow in poverty, and that . . . the adverse social impact on the affected communities far outweigh the gains promised by mining Trans-National Corporations (TNCs)."[57]

On July 5, 2000, the CBCP released the pastoral letter *Water Is Life*, which focused on the critical problem of water and the need to protect watersheds and aquifers. It called on the State to address conflicts in the National Integrated Protected Areas System Act (1992),[58] the Mining Act (1995) and

---

[56] CBCP, *What Is Happening to Our Beautiful Land?*

[57] CBCP, "A Statement of Concern on the Mining Act of 1995," 1998, http://www.no2miningph.org/wp/2011/10/22/cbcp-a-statement-of-concern-on-the-mining-act-of-1995/.

[58] The National Integrated Protected Areas System Act 1992 allows the conversion of indigenous lands into national parks and reserves for the purpose of ecotourism. This can lead to the prohibition of indigenous peoples to roam and harvest products in the forest.

the Indigenous Peoples' Rights Act (1997) in order for the community to be granted resource rights and responsibilities that do not jeopardize the rights of the lowlands and the succeeding generations. It warned that "it is not acceptable to continue to compromise the poor and marginalized in the interest of an economic growth that is not shared."[59]

In the 2006 pastoral letter *A Statement on Mining Issues and Concerns*, the CBCP called for the repeal of the Mining Act of 1995.[60] The tragic experience of environmental tragedies and incidents negated mining companies' assurance of sustainable and responsible mining.

The 2008 pastoral letter *Upholding the Sanctity of Life* dealt with the issues of irresponsible mining, illegal logging, and global warming and climate change. It called for a "moratorium on mining activities until the government and the mining companies learn to uphold the right of the indigenous peoples, compensate the affected communities for past damages, and ensure responsible mining practices." It reaffirmed that "we should learn from our Indigenous Filipinos who managed their forests in a sustainable way for hundreds and thousands of years."[61]

Other Local Church Initiatives

In addition to the CBCP pastoral letters, from 1997 to 2010, at least ten individuals or groups of bishops[62] had written to

---

[59] CBCP, *Water Is Life*, 2000, http://www.cbcponline.org/documents/2000s/2000-water_is_life.html.

[60] CBCP, *A Statement on Mining Issues and Concerns: Do Not Defile the Land Where You Live and Where I Dwell* (Num 35:34), 2006, http://www.cbcponline.net/documents/2000s/html/2006-AStatementonminingissuesandconcerns.html.

[61] CBCP, *Upholding the Sanctity of Life* (20 Years after the CBCP Pastoral Letter *What Is Happening to Our Beautiful Land?*), 2008, http://cbcpwebsite.com/2000s/2008/upholding.html.

[62] Jose S. Palma, DD, Emmanuel C. Trance, DD, et al., "A Call to Stop Mining in Eastern Visayas Region," 2010, http://www.philstar.com/letters-editor/625774/call-stop-mining-eastern-visayas-region.

shareholders of mining companies to stop their operations, and to the Roman Catholic Church in Canada (where the mining corporation is based) to protest discrimination against indigenous people. Others called for the repeal of the Mining Act of 1995, for a moratorium on new mining, or for a ban on mining in general. In 2010, the CBCP wrote a letter to former President Benigno Aquino questioning "the neoliberal pitch that there is no other path to development except through further economic liberalization, especially in the mining industry."[63] Since the president had created a Truth Commission for graft and corruption, the CBCP also called for a Truth Commission for environmental crimes that remained unpunished. In 2012, 72 out of the 98 members of the CBCP called on legislators to pass the Alternative Minerals Management Bill, which would allow mining only for local use, and would establish "no-go zones" such as ancestral lands of indigenous peoples, watersheds, and areas of biodiversity.

In addition to issuing pastoral letters, the church helps indigenous peoples through the diocesan social action centers throughout the country. Where there are IPs, the social action center has an indigenous desk that assists them in their struggles. Another means by which the church has helped is through a range of NGOs it has formed to assist IPs. The Subanen, for example, are assisted by the Dipolog-Iligan-Ozamis-Pagadian-Ipil-Marawi Committee on Mining Issues, an NGO created by the dioceses or prelatures of these places.

Other faiths in the Philippines, such as the United Church of Christ in the Philippines (UCCP) and the Iglesia Filipiniana Independiente, have also joined protests against the harassment, militarization, and massacre of members of indigenous groups who resist mining.[64] The UCCP's Haran Mission Cen-

---

[63] William Norman Holden, "Ecclesial Opposition to Large-Scale Mining on Samar: Neoliberalism Meets the Church of the Poor in a Wounded Land," *Religions* 3 (2012): 853.

[64] Iglesia Filipiniana Independiente, "End the Plunder of Nature, Stop

ter in Mindanao housed 700 displaced Lumads in 2016 before it was burned down by paramilitias.

Education and Cultural Development

The Protestant churches have also been very active in responding to the plight of IPs in the Philippines. The Integrated Development Program for Indigenous Peoples (IDPIP), a non-evangelical special development and service program for IPs under the United Church of Christ of the Philippines-Southern Luzon Jurisdictional Area, started when the Iraya Mangyans, the first IPs to organize into a tribal-wide federation in the country (in 1986), requested the UCCP's assistance in strengthening the federation. After the IDPIP's success in that effort, they expanded to help organize other IPs in the Southern Tagalog region. Their services include building schools where functional literacy, sanitation, and industrial skills are developed. The IDPIP heeds the call of the World Council of Churches to "support indigenous Peoples' right to self-determination with regard to their political and economic future, culture, land rights, spirituality, language, tradition, and forms of organization, and the protection of Indigenous Peoples' knowledge including intellectual property rights."[65]

As for the Catholic Church, in the first seven decades of the twentieth century, the interventions of Catholic religious congregations or Indigenous People's Apostolates (IPAs) were based on the colonial notion that the IPs needed to be civilized and assimilated within the mainstream society. In the 1980s the education content was contextualized, and a number of dioceses established dormitories exclusively for IPs in order to facilitate adjustment and lessen experiences of discrimination.

---

the Murder of Indigenous People," 2015, http://hkpinoytv.com/protest-action-against-lumad-killings/.

[65] World Council of Churches, "A Statement on Human Rights," Section 3.26: Rights of Indigenous Peoples, (Harare, Zimbabwe, December 1998), http://www.wcc-coe.org/wcc/assembly/hr-e.html.

However, their intervention was still aimed at integrating IPs into the mainstream society.

In 2002, the Episcopal Commission on Indigenous Peoples held the first national consultations on indigenous education. It became a forum for religious congregations and various IPAs to share their experiences and views. It became clear that education was alienating the indigenous youth from their communities, history, and heritage. The elders were worried about the fate of their ancestral domains if the next generation were to have no appreciation of their culture. The whole system needed to be recast toward a more culturally sensitive education, which some congregations and IPAs had already introduced in the 1980s. This type of education is different from past interventions in the following ways:

1. It is a form of decolonization that instills self-determination and values indigenous knowledge systems and practices.
2. It is community-based—the IPs themselves are involved in the youth education process.
3. It does not only focus on cultural manifestations such as songs, dances, and attires, but instead views culture as a living process. From this vantage point, it examines "how the cultural products came about, why they are changing, discussions on the impact of cultural change on communities and identity, the maintenance of intergenerational ties, etc. It is the understanding of cultural processes that will help indigenous youth to better understand why their community is what it is today and how to concretely maintain their community and culture as a living entity."[66]

---

[66] ECIP, "From Alienation to Rootedness: Taking on the Challenge of Reformulating Education Interventions with IP Communities," Philippines: A Consolidated Report by the Episcopal Commission on Indigenous Peoples, 2007.

4. It imparts knowledge and skills to help indigenous youth to engage in today's world as active participants in the shaping of the future. Education is important to sustainability as flourishing and the church, through the Episcopal Commission, is doing its part to encourage indigenous youth to appreciate their identity and care for their community.

For the IPs, land is central to their identity as a people. It not only nourishes them, but through it, they are connected to their ancestors and their spirits. In the name of development, an aggressive neoliberal, foreign-driven economic model has led to the destruction of their environment and a displacement from their ancestral lands tantamount to ethnocide.

Although the concept of sustainable development has been promoted to counter ecologically unsustainable practices and inequality, it has often been co-opted by businesses to hide their unsustainable practices. Even when understood correctly, it is confined to the material aspect of development. The indigenous peoples' perspective challenges us to expand this concept of sustainable development to include cultural, spiritual, and religious dimensions. This reframing may be expressed more fully by the concept of *sustainability as flourishing*— resulting from a care for nature, for each other, for ourselves, and for the spiritual or transcendent worlds. In *Laudato Si'*, this concept is expressed by the phrase "integral and sustainable development" and in the encyclical's emphasis on caring.

We have also shown how, in line with its vision of being a Church of the Poor, the local churches have been very actively engaged in the struggles of indigenous peoples toward sustainability and flourishing by helping them protect their ancestral domains, their environment, their rights, and their culture. In their advocacies, the local churches in the Philippines have provided examples of how to care for the earth and the poorest of the poor.

CHAPTER FIVE

Migrant Remittances as
Utang na Loob: *Virtues and Vices*

Transnational migration is a fertile ground for postcolonial reflection. The Philippines is among the top three remittance-receiving countries, with India first, followed by China.[1] Since an estimated 10 percent of families have a migrant relative abroad and each family consists of an average of five members, then at least fifty million (nearly half of the Philippine population) benefit from remittances. As an Asian Development Bank paper noted, "Remittances have become the single most important source of foreign exchange to the economy and a significant source of income for recipient families."[2]

This chapter examines migrant remittances as an expression of *utang na loob* (debt of solidarity). We expound a theology of gift premised on creation as God's gift (*kaloob*)—this theology describes our shared *loob* (inner self) with the rest of creation and notes our responsibility to honor our *utang na loob* to fellow humans and other co-creatures. We then delve into remittance as an expression of the virtue of *utang*

---

[1] Migration and Remittances Factbook 2016 (World Bank), http://www.worldbank.org/en/research/brief/migration-and-remittances.

[2] Alvin P. Yang, Guntur Sugiyarto, and Shikha Jha, "Remittances and Household Behavior in the Philippines," Asian Development Bank, 2009, https://www.adb.org/publications/remittances-and-household-behavior-philippines.

na loob, discuss the correlative vices, and conclude by highlighting some solidarity initiatives toward virtuous structures.[3]

Remittance in the Context of a Gift Economy

A gift economy is an economy based on giving within the context of relationships, which are either contemporary or dating back to ancient times.[4] It is different from barter or commercial economies, in which goods or labor are exchanged with something of equal monetary worth. It is the economy of ancient societies before money was used, and it was expressed in various cultural forms such as in the Kula in New Guinea, as described by Marcel Mauss.[5] The Kula is a system involving the exchange of non-economic goods among twenty or so islands on the eastern side of New Guinea. It fosters social bonds between donor and donee and lays the groundwork for future economic exchanges. Giving is an altruistic gesture toward a recipient; however, the giver also benefits in terms of increased social capital and support from other members of the community in times of need.

Genevieve Vaughan, in *Women and the Gift Economy: A Radically Different Worldview Is Possible*, argued that the gift economy is gendered.[6] Women are socialized more into this paradigm, which values giving and nurturing. Much of the

---

[3] The shift to the discourse from values to virtues in the Philippines, especially in the field of theology, can be credited to the influence of renowned virtue ethicist James F. Keenan who has mentored a number of Philippine moral theologians.

[4] Charles Eisenstein, *Sacred Economics: Money, Gift, and Society in the Age of Transition* (Berkeley, CA: North Atlantic Books, 2011). There has been a surge of interest in the appropriation of the traditional gift economy operative in ancient societies, as an alternative to neoliberal capitalist economies for the twenty-first century as exemplified in this book.

[5] Marcel Mauss, *The Gift: Forms and Functions of Exchange in Archaic Societies* (London: Cohen & West, 1970).

[6] Genevieve Vaughan, *Women and the Gift Economy: A Radically Different Worldview Is Possible* (Toronto: Inanna Publications, 2007).

caretaking work done in families is based on the principle of the gift economy.[7] Examples of this include parents working hard to raise and educate their children, and adult children taking care of their parents.

In this section, I discuss migrant remittance in the context of the Philippine gift economy, but before proceeding, let us first identify the different types of remittances.

Types of Remittances

There are two main types of remittance—the personal remittance and the social remittance. Personal remittances are the sum of the employee's wage, personal transfers, capital transfers, and social benefits. If a migrant has lived in a host country for one year or longer, he or she is considered a resident regardless of immigration status; and what he or she sends to the home country in cash or in kind is considered a personal transfer. This thus includes not only money but also goods, such as those placed inside the iconic *balikbayan* or "homecoming" box. Overseas Philippine workers usually keep an open balikbayan box that they slowly fill with goods like chocolates, sneakers, clothes, and bags from the host country; when filled, the bag is sent duty-free via a shipping courier.

Capital transfers in kind are transfers of ownership of non-financial assets or cancellation of debt. For example, Luna is a Filipina domestic helper in the UK. She had paid the mortgage for a house in the Philippines for her sister, who probably took care of her kids when they were still there and Luna was working abroad. In addition, she purchased a fourteen-hectare coconut plantation for her father. The amount she spent to pay for her sister's house and to buy the coconut plantation for her father are considered capital transfers. Social security

---

[7] In contrast, Vaughan posits that the exchange paradigm is more reflective of male socialization and the values expressed in competition and domination.

and pension funds that the migrant can enjoy even as he or she goes back to the home country constitute the "social benefits" portion of one's personal remittances.

The sociologist Peggy Levitt, in her 2001 book, *The Transnational Villagers*, coined the term *social remittances* to refer to nonmonetary remittance flows from migrants—e.g., norms, practices, identities, and social capital—which may or may not be beneficial to the home country or to the host country.[8]

Social remittances can be classified into three, often intersecting, types:[9] (1) *Cultural* social remittances refer to cross-cultural exchange (e.g., values and religious/cultural practices) between the migrant's multiple homelands. One example is how migrants are making the churches in developed nations vibrant again, and bringing along with them popular religious practices. (2) *Ecological* social remittances refer to the civic participation or community development projects of migrants. The contribution of overseas Philippine workers to the development of a village in Mabini, Batangas, called Pulong Anahao, is an example of an ecological social remittance. Pulong Anahao is now more popularly known as Little Italy because 25 percent of the residents work in Italy; from the fruits of their labor, they have built houses of Mediterranean pastel-colored style schools, region-wide water supply schemes, roads,

---

[8] Peggy Levitt, *The Transnational Villagers* (Berkeley: University of California Press, 2001), 54–69. See also Peggy Levitt and Deepak Lamba-Nieves, "'It's Not Just about the Economy, Stupid'—Social Remittances Revisited," May 21, 2010, http://www.migrationpolicy.org/article/its-not-just-about-economy-stupid-social-remittances-revisited. For example, after accumulating a great deal of informal cultural capital related to her humanitarian social remittances, Aurora has also attained the necessary professional accreditation to be qualified as a social worker if she returns home.

[9] For other cases of migrants' investments, migrant giving, and partnerships between overseas Filipinos-Philippine institutions, see Maruja M. B. Asis, Fabio Baggio, Jose Maria de Jesus Palabrica, and Golda Myra Roma, *Transnational Bridges: Migration, Development and Solidarity in the Philippines* (Metro-Manila: Scalabrini Migration Center and Commission on Filipinos Overseas, 2010).

and other infrastructure, endeavors that are normally prime mandates for the local government. Through their assistance, the Mabini municipality in 2009 leaped from a third-class to a first-class municipality in a government ranking of towns nationwide.[10] The migrant workers likewise financed the feasts held annually, taking over the sponsorship previously shouldered by local entrepreneurs, churches, and municipalities. (3) *Political* social remittances refer to the migrants' political activism in the host and home country. One example is the transnational activism of the NGOs Mission for Migrant Workers and Asian Migrant Centre that spans Hong Kong and the Philippines, advocating for the rights of Philippine workers and later of other nationalities as well.[11]

Social remittances circulate "when migrants return to live in or visit their communities of origin; when nonmigrants visit their friends and family in a receiving country; or through letters, videos, e-mails, blogs, and phone calls."[12]

Utang na Loob:
The Philippine Gift Economy

Some authors think in binary terms in the effort to understand whether remittances are done from altruistic motives or from self-interest. In the context of the Philippine culture, a fruitful way of understanding remittances is from the perspective of a gift economy.

The main category in the Philippine gift economy is *utang na loob*. *Utang na loob* is literally translated as "debt of the inner self," but it is more commonly understood as a debt

---

[10] "Many OFW Dream Houses in Little Italy Still Empty," *Philippine Daily Inquirer*, September 20, 2010, https://www.pressreader.com/philippines/philippine-daily-inquirer/20100920/282862252217932.

[11] See also Ma. Glenda Lopez Wui and Dina Delias, "Examining the Struggles for Domestic Workers: Hong Kong and the Philippines as Interacting Sites of Activism," *Philippine Political Science Journal*, 36, no. 2 (2015): 190–208.

[12] Levitt and Lamba-Nieves, "It's Not Just about the Economy."

of reciprocity.[13] Influenced by Western-oriented approaches, social scientists in the Philippines in the mid-twentieth century interpreted reciprocity in *utang na loob* from a mercantilist perspective. The recipient expresses his or her gratitude by returning the favor with something worth the same amount, or with interest.[14]

This reciprocity discourse on *utang na loob* can have a domesticating effect because it is usually the poor who become recipients of charity from the rich and are thereby obligated to pay back the benefactor out of gratitude, thus keeping them subject to power-wielding authorities.[15] Furthermore, if this is the only meaning of *utang na loob*, then there is no more need to add *loob* (inner self) to it; *utang* (debt) would suffice.[16] Others highlight the fact that no amount of money can ever repay an *utang na loob*. As Filipino philosopher-anthropologist Albert Alejo underlines, "*Ang utang na loob ay hindi binabayaran kundi tinatanaw o kinikilala. . . . Inaalala ito ng tumanggap ngunit kinakalimutan ng nagbigay. Mas magandang sabihing sinusuklian ito, at hindi binabayaran.*"[17] ("Debt of human solidarity is not paid but instead acknowledged. . . . It is recognized by the recipient but forgotten by the giver. It

---

[13] See Francis Dancel, "*Utang na Loob* [Debt of Goodwill]: A Philosophical Analysis," in *Filipino Cultural Traits: Claro R. Ceniza Lectures*, ed. Rolando M. Gripaldo, vol. 4, *Cultural Heritage and Contemporary Change* (Manila: CRVP, 2005), 109–28.

[14] Mary Racelis Hollnsteiner, "Reciprocity in the Lowland Philippines," in *Four Readings on Philippine Values*, ed. Frank Lynch and A. de Guzman II (Metro-Manila: Ateneo de Manila University Press, 1970), 69.

[15] Virgilio Enriquez, "*Pakikisama o Pakikibaka*: Understanding the Psychology of the Filipino," paper read at the conference on Philippine Culture, Bay Area Bilingual Education League, Berkeley, California, April 29–30, 1977.

[16] Reynaldo Clemeña Ileto, *Pasyon and Revolution: Popular Movements in the Philippines 1840–1910* (Metro-Manila: Ateneo de Manila University Press, 1979), 230.

[17] Albert Alejo, *Tao po Tuloy! Isang Landas ng Pag-unawa sa Loob ng Tao* (Manila: Office of Research and Publications, 1990), 151.

is better to say that one is giving back the change instead of repaying.")

Some authors also translate *utang na loob* as a debt of gratitude. But although there is a behavioral resemblance between the two, *utang na loob* is more than just gratitude. *Utang na loob* is more emotionally charged than gratitude, and although the latter is basically linked to positive feelings, *utang na loob* can be positively or negatively construed based on the context.[18] Furthermore, gratitude from the recipient is usually expected *after* a good deed has been performed. *Utang na loob*, as the Filipino theologian José M. de Mesa indicated, functions "prior to any reception of favor. It is used as a plea prior to any favor because *utang na loob*, the debt owed to another person who shares a common humanity (*loob*), exists just because we are fellow human beings."[19] This meaning is highlighted when *utang na loob* is used as a final appeal. A woman who is about to be raped prefaces her plea with "*Utang na loob!*" The plea is made to appeal to the common humanity, the common "*loob*" she and her assailant share. *Utang na loob* is founded not in the exchange of favors but in the commitment to "human solidarity." It is ultimately situated within the belief that all of life is a gift (our Filipino word for gift is *kaloob*, meaning shared inner self). If life is a gift (*kaloob*) from God, this means we all share in God's loob or inner self. A person with *utang na loob* acknowledges this and reciprocates with gratitude, knowing that he or she cannot fully repay the gift.

The reciprocation here need not be to the person who has done the favor; it can be paid forward in tangible or intangible ways to others who are in need, which is another indication that utang na loob goes beyond gratitude and is instead a debt of human solidarity.

---

18 Dancel, "*Utang na loob*," 109–28.

19 José M. de Mesa, *Solidarity with the Culture: Studies in Theological Re-rooting* (Metro-Manila: Maryhill School of Theology, 1987), 37.

Remittances as Expression of Utang na Loob

Several writings have linked the felt duty, especially of daughters, to send remittances to their families as an expression of *utang na loob*.[20] Traditionally, the expectation is for the youngest daughter to take care of her parents or the elderly in the family, while the eldest siblings are in charge of the younger ones. The obligation to remit oftentimes causes marital problems for women in intermarriages abroad. Husbands from other cultures may find it difficult to understand why their wives continue to help their families financially, including their siblings and other relatives.[21] One can only understand this from within the culture emphasizing the strong bond that links the family: the Filipino word for sibling is *kapatid* (cut from the same body) and for relatives is *kamaganak* (literally translated as shared family).

Remittance is not only an expression of *utang na loob* when done for one's family of origin but also when done for one's children. Compared to women, migrant men, as expected breadwinners for their families, are more likely to remit for their spouse and children.[22] As earlier noted, *utang na loob* is

---

[20] Claudia Liebelt, *Caring for the "Holy Land": Filipina Domestic Workers in Israel* (New York: Berghahn, 2011); Lillian Trager, *The City Connection: Migration and Family Interdependence in the Philippines* (Ann Arbor: University of Michigan Press, 1988).

[21] Nicole Woelz-Stirling, Lenore Manderson, Margaret Kelaher, and Sara Gordon, "Marital Conflict and Finances among Filipinas in Australia," *International Journal of Intercultural Relations* 24, no. 6 (November 2000): 791–805. This study reveals that women generally send money for the education of younger siblings and to finance medical expenses of the family. The felt obligation to remit stops when these needs have been addressed.

[22] Steven McKay, "'So They Remember Me When I'm Gone': Remittances, Fatherhood and Gender Relations of Filipino Migrant Men," in *Transnational Labour Migration, Remittances and the Changing Family in Asia*, ed. Lan Anh Hoang and Brenda S. A. Yeoh (New York: Palgrave Macmillan, 2015), 111.

owed prior to the reception of any favors because it is basically a debt of human solidarity. It is "paid forward" to one's children—a way of circulating the gift. In relation to this, some sociologists view remittance as a commodification of love, as a way to "buy love."[23] Certainly, the capitalist consumerist culture has influenced the way migrants and their children think. But from the perspective of the migrants, remittance is also the most tangible evidence that migrants do not break ties with their countries or communities of origin even as they migrate. It is symbolic of the reality that the people left behind are still in the consciousness and the loving memory of the migrant.

Marian, who was interviewed by Claudia Liebelt, is a fifty-seven-year-old domestic helper, who was married to an Israeli who passed away early in their marriage.[24] She comes from a family of eight, most of whom are now poor urban settlers in Metro Manila. Even if several of them work abroad, she is the only one who "made it"—the only one who owns a house, holds a Western (Israeli) citizenship, and has a stable job. She tells of how her extended family often asks her for money. With limited cash, she had to decide how much to give. She felt guilty when her brother died because the family could not afford an operation to save his life. Even as her daughter is embarrassed to bring her friends to their house because of their humble means in Israel, "she still [feels] an obligation to support her family financially nearly three decades after leaving the Philippines." She is "proud to be one of the family's major supporters" and to be "elevated in her social position even if she is the youngest."[25]

Liebelt pointed out that because migrants are living in an environment of racial discrimination and subhuman labor

---

[23] Eileen Boris and Rhacel Salazar Parreñas, eds., *Intimate Labors: Cultures, Technologies, and the Politics of Care* (Stanford, CA: Stanford University Press, 2010), 1.

[24] Liebelt, *Caring for the "Holy Land,"* 69.

[25] Ibid., 68.

conditions, their self-esteem is elevated by their ability to help others who are in greater need. She compared this dynamic to that of Haitian migrants for whom their "humanity is defined by their acts of [financially] helping others." She suspected rightly that in the case of Marian, her "helping was similarly connected to her idea of being human."[26] Her generosity, in Philippine categories, is an expression of *utang na loob*—her debt of human solidarity.

Utang na loob as debt of solidarity is passed on to children and exerts a strong pressure as a social and moral filial obligation. For example, Batang Atikha Savers Club, a children's money-saving project initiated by Atikha, a Philippine NGO in San Pablo City, Laguna, teaches Philippine children left behind by migrants to acknowledge their *utang na loob* through responsible use of resources, behaving well, and assuming their parents' duties in their absence.[27]

Social remittance is also an expression of the debt of solidarity to one's community/home and to one's host country. For instance, Filipinos in the San Francisco Bay Area helped repair the St. Thomas the Apostle Church in the Philippines, while also contributing to the renovation of Saint Boniface Church in San Francisco in the United States. They donated to disaster relief efforts not only in their home provinces but also to the victims of Hurricane Katrina, one of the deadliest US hurricanes in history.[28] Their *utang na loob* or debt of human solidarity has thus gone beyond their family and nation of origin.

---

[26] Ibid.

[27] Cheryl Alipio, "Filipino Children and the Affective Economy of Saving and Being Saved: Remittances and Debts in Transnational Migrant Families," in *Transnational Labour Migration, Remittances and the Changing Family in Asia*, ed. Lan Anh Hoang and Brenda S. A. Yeoh (New York: Palgrave Macmillan, 2015), 227–56.

[28] Joaquin Jay Gonzalez, *Filipino American Faith in Action: Immigration, Religion, and Civic Engagement* (New York: New York University Press, 2009), 78.

Utang na Loob and a Theology of Gift

Filipino theologian Edmundo Pacifico Guzman further developed the concept of *utang na loob* to include "debt of our Earthly solidarity" on account of creation as God's *kaloob* (gift).[29] For Guzman, *utang na loob*, or debt of solidarity with all of creation, is premised on creation as God's *kaloob*. *Ka* is a Filipino prefix that means "to share with." Thus, *kaloob* (gift) is literally translated as shared inner self. The gift is an extension of the giver's self. Creation as God's *kaloob* (gift) suggests that creation shares in the inner self or depths of God. Though this may seem to imply that the world emanated from God, the second-century church fathers stressed that the world was created by God out of nothing (ex nihilo).[30] Creation as gift of God is a sacrament of the divine. It shares in the divine self (implying panentheism) but is not equivalent to God's self (which would imply pantheism). As Guzman further argued, "In its capacity also as a cultural metaphor based on *loob* [inner self] the meaning of and import of *utang na loob* can be stretched in order to express that gratitude we have for nature and the Earth which we can experience as *kaloob* [gift; shared inner self] to us."[31] Flowing forth from God's *kagandahang-loob* (gracious goodness), the whole

---

[29] Edmundo Pacifico Guzman, "Creation as God's Kaloob: Towards an Ecological Theology of Creation in the Lowland Filipino Socio-cultural Context," Part II (PhD diss., Catholic University of Louvain, 1995), 394–448. A later theologizing on creation as gift and our debt of responsibility to humans and creation can be found in Martin M. Lintner, OSM, "Dono e debito, tra scienze umane e teologia: Prospettiva etico-teologica," Dell'ufficio Nazionale per i Problemi Sociali e il Lavoro e del Servizio Nazionale per il Progetto Culturale, 7 (February 2013): 36.

[30] Leo Scheffcyck, *Creation and Providence*, trans. Richard Strachan (New York: Herder and Herder, 1970), 47–64.

[31] Guzman, "Creation as God's Kaloob," 438.

of creation is sacred. With this creation with which we share our giftedness and participation in the divine loob, we express our debt of human and earthly solidarity.

Moral theologian Brian Johnstone likewise develops a theology of gift, this time in critical dialogue with philosophers such as Jacques Derrida, who removed any element of reciprocity from his discourse on gift because of how that concept can be manipulated to express commercial exchange and exclusion of the other.[32]

Derrida spoke of the "impossibility" or, more accurately, the "cancellation" of a gift: "as soon as a gift is identified as a gift, with the meaning of a gift, then it is cancelled as a gift. It is reintroduced into the circle of exchange and destroyed as a gift."[33] The giver looks good and the recipient of a gift in turn gets indebted, which is the reverse of what a gift should accomplish. This economic exchange is transcended only if I "refer the gift to the other." The example Derrida gave to illustrate such a referral is Abraham's sacrifice of Isaac.[34] God's decision to spare the life of Isaac is an absolute gift, a reward to Abraham, who in turn "has renounced absolutely any economy of reward."[35] For Derrida, to refer the gift to the other means to attribute the gift to God.

Johnstone qualified, though, that for Derrida, God is not a personal God but is located within the human subject. Johnstone's Christian alternative is to draw more from scriptural and theological resources that refer to a personal God, an

---

[32] Brian Johnstone, "The Ethics of the Gift: According to Aquinas, Derrida and Marion," *Australian Journal of Theology* 3 (August 2004): 1–16.

[33] "On the Gift: A Discussion between Jacques Derrida and Jean-Luc Marion," moderated by Richard Kearney, in *God, the Gift, and Postmodernism*, ed. John D. Caputo and Michael J. Scanlon (Bloomington: Indiana University Press, 1999), 59.

[34] Jacques Derrida, *The Gift of Death* (Chicago: University of Chicago Press, 1995), 53–81.

[35] Johnstone, "The Ethics of the Gift," 9.

absolute Other, and that demonstrate the reciprocity between Jesus and the Father.

Johnstone pointed out that from a Christian notion of creation ex nihilo, being itself is a gift. This idea is similar to Guzman's theology of creation as *kaloob* or gift. The self and the other, both of whom receive being as a gift, are thus integrally linked to each other and are themselves potential givers. The similarity of the self and the other here does not erase their difference. Johnstone notes that an important fulcrum for philosophers of gift is the relation of the self to the other, where the other should neither be subsumed to the self nor the self subsumed to the other. A related concern is the relation of the object and the subject of a gift. Following Karol Wojtyla (later Pope John Paul II), for whom it is through action that the boundary between subject and object is overcome,[36] Johnstone argued that it is the act of giving and receiving that transcends the separation of the subject (giver) and the object (gift). In Philippine categories, this is easily understood since the gift (object) is a *kaloob*—sharing in the depths or inner self of the giver (subject).

Johnstone illustrated how the boundaries between self and other, giver and gift, are transcended, and also how reciprocity can still exist in the act of gift-giving by referring to the self-sacrifice of Jesus. In Matthew 26:39, Jesus cried out, "My Father, if it is possible, let this cup pass from me; yet not what I want but what you want."[37] The phrase "yet not what I want but what you want" suggests a difference in what Jesus and the Father desire, though this leads to total acceptance later on Jesus's part (an acceptance that nevertheless does not obliterate

---

[36] Karol Wojtyla, *The Acting Person* (Dordrecht: Springer, 1979).

[37] In John 10:18, Jesus said: "For this reason the Father loves me, because I lay down my life in order to take it up again. No one takes it from me, but I lay it down of my own accord. I have power to lay it down, and I have power to take it up again. I have received this command from my Father."

this difference). Moreover, Jesus laid down his life as participation in the divine love that is self-giving. The goal in both Abraham and Jesus is participation in God's faithfulness or self-giving, which is the reward in itself.

In Luke 6:32–36, Jesus says: "If you love those who love you, what credit is that to you? . . . But love your enemies, do good, and lend, expecting nothing in return." This is similar to *utang na loob* as a virtue—forgotten by the giver but acknowledged by the receiver. The text continues: "Your reward will be great, and you will be children of the Most High. . . . Be merciful, just as your Father is merciful." The ultimate "reward" is in becoming a child of God or sharing in the image of God, the giver.

It is thus possible to reciprocate a gift without undermining the notion of gift. Jesus did not give his life to others to get a reward, but the resurrection's reward is a participation in that divine giving. This is in line with Thomas Aquinas's understanding of gift as linked to grace, that is, as thanksgiving for the gift received. This is not a payback but rather the "full actualizing of the gift-giving. One's giving thanks in recompense is itself a further receiving, and what is received is participation in the gift-giving of the Word and the Spirit."[38] Johnstone's theology of gift also echoes the view of Jean-Luc Marion, Catholic philosopher of gift, that Jesus's self-giving is motivated not by hope of reward but by participation or imitation of the ultimate giver (God), in the divine exchange. The gift goes beyond the economic circle, and it is this excess that interests Marion.[39]

---

[38] Thomas Aquinas closely linked gift to "grace" in its three senses. The first sense refers to the love (*dilectio*) of another. This is what is implied when somebody says "one enjoys the good will (grace) of another." A second sense is the gift itself: a "gratuitous gift" (*donum gratis datum*). The third sense is gratitude for the gift that is received. Johnstone, "The Ethics of the Gift," 14.

[39] Lintner, "Dono o e debito."

Utang na Loob as a Virtue

There are similarities in Guzman's concept of *utang na loob* and Johnstone's notion of gift-giving and receiving as participation in divine self-giving. *Gift* is translated in Filipino as *kaloob* (shared inner self). Creation as gift or God's *kaloob* shares with us the inner self of God. *Utang na loob* as debt of solidarity is a form of self-gift; it recognizes our oneness or union with the needs of the other and, at a deeper level, our common humanity and creatureliness. *Utang na loob* as debt of human and earthly solidarity situates a person within a circle of interdependence that re-creates divine self-giving and receiving.

Utang na loob is a character trait of one who acknowledges his or her life as a gift (*kaloob*) in a web of interdependence within the family/community/society/creation. This obliges the person to reciprocate by offering a gift to others as a debt of solidarity to fellow humans as well as with creation. Remittance is a gift that is not a mere commodity; it is a *kaloob*, part of the loob of the giver, which elicits *utang na loob*, a debt of the inner self, on the part of the receiver. It goes beyond economic exchange because, ideally, it is forgotten by the giver but acknowledged by the receiver.

Correlative Virtues

Thomas Aquinas held that a true virtue is connected with other virtues. We have already discussed how honoring one's *utang na loob* as a character disposition is tied to the virtue of generosity. For migrants, it is also linked to sacrifice, solidarity, and good stewardship. Pinky from "Little Italy" remits money monthly to her parents and provides support from time to time to her nonmigrant siblings and their families. She muses,

The [domestic] work itself is not difficult. What is hard is what you feel in your heart [loob] if there are problems here in the Philippines. For example, if your budget is not enough and someone here is sick. You want to help but you cannot: that is a very heavy burden that I carry in my heart [loob].[40]

To respond to the needs of her family, she gets extra work, saves on personal needs like food, and even takes out loans from a relative or her employer.

Recipients of remittance, in turn, can express their utang na loob through good stewardship. A Christian steward receives a gift with gratitude, responsibly tends it, and shares it justly with others.

Utang na Loob *Guided by Prudence*

In Liebelt's discussions with women migrant workers in Israel, the interviewees narrated many stories of tensions and betrayals in the use of hard-earned money for things that are not necessary.[41] Furthermore, the cost of bringing "pasalubong" or gift remittance (in kind) often dissuades migrants from coming home more often, due to the high economic cost of such visits. The migrant is expected not only to bring gifts but also to finance large social gatherings in the home community.

There can be no excess, however, of *utang na loob* as debt of human solidarity. Aristotle contended that virtue in itself cannot be excessive, but that it should be guided by prudence.[42] Practical wisdom involves being aware of the consequences of

---

[40] Quoted in Evangeline O. Katigbak, "Moralizing Emotional Remittances: Transnational Familyhood and Translocal Moral Economy in the Philippines' 'Little Italy,'" *Global Networks* 15, no. 4 (2015): 527.

[41] See, for instance, the story of Marian in Liebelt, *Caring for the "Holy Land,"* 68–69.

[42] *Aristotle's Ethics: Writings from the Complete Works*, rev. ed., ed. Jonathan Barnes and Anthony Kenny (Princeton, NJ: Princeton University Press, 2014), 10.

one's deeds, establishing priorities, and discerning the virtuous mean in particular contexts.[43]

In *The Nicomachean Ethics*, Aristotle pointed out that a generous person "will give to the right people, the right amount, at the right time."[44] Since generosity is a key element in *utang na loob*, it is important to ask if a migrant is giving the right amount, given his or her capacity, to the right people (those who are truly needy). Regarding the latter, both St. Augustine and St. Thomas Aquinas underlined our duty as Christians to love everyone. However, Aquinas states that there is an *ordo amoris* or "order of priorities among diverse loves," with particular treatment proper to those with whom we are specially related, such as parents and spouses.[45]

Utang na Loob *and Self-Care*

Another virtue that has to guide *utang na loob* is self-care. Self-care includes the development of self-esteem, the promotion of one's health, and protecting oneself from being taken advantage of by others.[46]

---

[43] "Virtue Ethics," *Stanford Encyclopedia of Philosophy*, https://plato.stanford.edu/entries/ethics-virtue/#Virt.

[44] Aristotle, *Nicomachean Ethics*, trans. with introduction and notes by Martin Oswald (New York: Macmillan Publications, 1962; reprint ed. 1989), 84. "A generous act does not depend on the amount given, but on the characteristic of the giver, and this makes him give relative to his property." Ibid., 85.

[45] David Hollenbach, SJ, "A Future beyond Borders: Reimagining the Nation-State and the Church," in *Living with(out) Borders: Catholic Theological Ethics on the Migrations of People*s, ed. Agnes M. Brazal and Maria Teresa Davila (Maryknoll, NY: Orbis Books, 2016), 228; see Aquinas, *Summa Theologiae* II–II, q. 26, arts. 6–8.

[46] See James F. Keenan, SJ, "Proposing Cardinal Virtues," *Theological Studies* 56, no. 4 (1995): 709–29; Daniel J. Harrington, SJ, and James F. Keenan, SJ, *Paul and Virtue Ethics: Building Bridges between New Testament Studies* (Lanham, MD: Rowman and Littlefield, 2010), 209; see also Stephen J. Pope, *The Evolution of Altruism and the Ordering of Love*

Self-care is something that is not often in the minds of Philippine overseas contract workers (OCW). Many give everything without reserving anything for their future. A 2015 survey revealed that only two in every five OCWs were able to save from their earnings.[47] Others are not only unable to save but they also fall into debt in order to support their families back home.[48]

Correlative Vices: The Lack and Excesses Related to *Utang na Loob*

Thomas underlined that "moral virtue is a habit of choosing the mean."[49] The mean is that which is between "doing or feeling too little and doing or feeling too much." If *pagtanaw ng utang na loob* is the mean, the excessive extreme would be the absence of *utang na loob* or being prodigal—being mindless with the use of money. The other extreme in terms of lack would be stinginess on the part of the migrant and dependency on the part of the recipient.

Shamelessness/Absence of Utang na Loob

In the Philippines, one who is devoid of *utang na loob* is considered a person of bad character, a person without shame (*walang hiya*). *Hiya* is an embodied sensitivity to one's *kapwa*

(Washington, DC: Georgetown University Press, 1994), and "Expressive Individualism and True Self Love: A Thomistic Perspective," *Journal of Religion* 71, no. 3 (1991): 384–99.

[47] "2015 Survey on Overseas Filipinos," Philippine Statistics Authority, 2016, https://psa.gov.ph/content/2015-survey-overseas-filipinos-0.

[48] Charito Basa, Violeta de Guzman, and Sabrina Marchetti, *International Migration and Over-indebtedness: The Case of Filipino Workers in Italy* (London: International Institute for Environment and Development, 2012).

[49] Aristotle, *The Nicomachean Ethics* ii, 6, cited by Thomas, ST II–I, q. 64, art. 1. See also Aristotle, book 2 of *The Nicomachean Ethics*, trans. with notes by Harris Rackham (Hertfordshire: Wordsworth, 1996), 35.

(fellow human). "The worst thing one can say about a person is that he or she is without shame (*walang hiya*), which is the same as to say that the person is *walang utang na loob*, without any sense of indebtedness."[50] Filipinos greatly resent being called shameless.[51] It is almost equivalent to being in a state of mortal sin in the Philippine context, as it alienates the person from his or her community.

The failure of the migrant to reciprocate *utang na loob* can happen as a result of being prodigal, such as spending one's income mindlessly either for oneself or for others. Being prodigal on the part of the recipient of remittance can mean spending the remittance on consumer goods that are not necessary, without regard for the hard work exerted by the giver in earning the money.

However, the discourse of the Philippine revolutionary group Katipunan on *utang na loob* shows that breaking ties of indebtedness (with a prodigal recipient) can be justified in certain cases. A poem by Procopio Bonifacio, the brother of Philippine national hero Andres Bonifacio, speaks of the Filipino as a child separating from its mother Spain because of her neglect and lack of motherly care.[52] The mother-child relationship is often linked by love and *utang na loob*. But the time had come to separate and break the bond because of the suffering mother Spain had caused. One can say that the circle of mutual indebtedness and participation in the divine self-giving is broken by those who abuse either the giver or the recipient and that in such instances, breaking the ties may indeed be called for.

---

[50] Vicente L. Rafael, *Contracting Colonialism: Translation and Christian Conversion in Tagalog Society under Early Spanish Rule* (Ithaca, NY: Cornell University Press, 1988), 127; see the discussion on hiya (shame) as a virtue in Chapter 6.

[51] Leonardo Mercado, *Elements of Filipino Philosophy* (Tacloban: Divine Word University Publ., 1974), 65.

[52] Ileto, *Pasyon and Revolution*, 103–5.

Family/National Dependency

Another vice that remittances can create is the serious problem of dependency. Instead of looking for jobs, some dependents simply wait for the remittance, thus limiting their productivity and contribution to the workforce.[53] If the migrant loses his or her job and is unable to send any more money or goods, everyone suffers—including the migrant.

On the national level, remittances have been keeping the Philippine economy afloat, especially during the periods of the Asian and global economic crises in 1997 and 2008, respectively. This may have been counterproductive since instead of pursuing economic reforms, the Philippine government simply relied on remittances to survive.

Some have argued, however, that even if remittances have not been used for investment in national development, the fact that they have been spent in part on human resource development such as better food and housing and education of children is tantamount to an investment for posterity. The investment in education and national development is, however, occluded by the migration mentality inculcated among children of migrants. A 2003 survey in the Philippines showed that 60 percent of children of overseas foreign workers expressed their plans to work abroad and the priority they would give to taking courses needed to thrive in the countries of the North rather than to courses needed to thrive in Philippines. And although they aspire to go to college, they are also aware that they could earn higher salaries abroad even without having a college diploma.[54]

There are also criticisms of migrants' use of remittances as consumerist and not directed toward a stable income in order to end the migration cycle. Although the use of

---

[53] See comment of Mayor of Little Italy, in "Many OFW Dream Houses in Little Italy Still Empty."

[54] Country Migration Report: The Philippines 2013 (Metro-Manila: International Organization for Migration/Scalabrini Migration Center, 2013).

remittances for investment is indeed low, attention should be directed at the larger economic context. The control of businesses, particularly in agriculture by rich and political families, prevents migrants from investing in small and medium enterprises.

Neoliberal Capitalism as Structure of Vice

Just as there are vices on the personal level, there also exist structures of vice on the societal level. Daniel Daly defines structures of vice "as social structures that in some way consistently function to prevent the human good, the common good, and human happiness, and, the socially rooted moral habits willingly internalized by moral agents that consistently prescribe sinful human acts, and produce human unhappiness."[55] Neoliberal capitalism is a structure of vice that breeds poverty and climate change, which are forces that push people to migrate. The lack of debt of human solidarity (*utang na loob*) is built within this social structure.

Although it is true that migration is an integral part of globalization, it is at the same time undeniable that a major factor in the massive migration from South to North is the impact of structural adjustment programs imposed by the World Bank and the International Monetary Fund (IMF) to indebted developing countries.[56]

In the 1970s, saturated with petro dollars from the Middle East and eager to make profits, the Western banks (including US banks) ignored traditional process and care in lending as they competed with one another to attract creditor nations,

[55] Daniel J. Daly, "Structures of Virtue and Vice," *New Blackfriars* 92 (2011): 341–57.

[56] Raúl Delgado Wise and Humberto Marquez Covarrubias, "The Dialectic between Uneven Development and Forced Migration: Toward a Political Economy Framework," in *The Migration—Development Nexus: Towards a Transnational Perspective*, ed. T. Faist, M. Fauser, and P. Kivisto (Basingstoke: Palgrave Macmillan, 2011), 187.

even those run by dictatorships like that of Ferdinand Marcos in the Philippines. When the United States raised interest rates in 1980 to around 20 percent, the indebted countries could not pay their debts. The IMF was tasked with making sure that these nations would pay in order to save the banks. Debtor countries could borrow more money, but this time they needed to follow IMF's structural adjustment program. The program's prescriptions included: (1) increasing exports; (2) abolishing subsidies (e.g., for farmers); (3) reducing public spending (e.g., on health, education, and social services); (4) reducing taxes on corporate profits (to attract foreign investments); and (5) deregulating working hours and wage agreements (e.g., scrapping minimum wage laws). In short—earn more and spend less, so that the country can pay their debts. The export orientation imposed on these countries actually prevented the diversification of their products, which could have made them less vulnerable to the reduction of prices of raw commodities in relation to higher-value-added goods and services. The inability to compete against imports led to the closure of some industries and the displacement of workers, who in turn looked for alternative means of livelihood abroad. For Filipino social activist and academic Walden Bello, the radical free trade policies started in the Philippines not with the founding of the World Trade Organization (WTO) in 1995, but with the IMF-imposed liberalization of the economy of around ninety developing countries a decade earlier.[57] As the papal encyclical *Sollicitudo Rei Socialis* correctly noted, "Through this mechanism [of debts], the means intended for the development of peoples has turned into a brake upon development instead, and indeed in some cases has even aggravated underdevelopment" (no. 19).[58] The 1980s has been

---

[57] Walden Bello, "How to Manufacture a Global Food Crisis: Lessons from the World Bank, IMF, and WTO," 2018, https://www.tni.org/es/node/10827.

[58] Pope John Paul II, *Sollicitudo Rei Socialis*, December 1987.

called the "lost decade" in Latin America. In a situation similar to that in Mexico with its reduced subsidies to corn farmers, the Philippines was reduced from being an exporter of rice, its staple food, to becoming the world's largest importer of rice. The Filipino people have been paying the debts incurred under the late dictator Marcos for thirty years now, and are bound to do so until 2025.

Furthermore, the capitalist mode of economic development has been a major cause of climate change, which has recently driven migration as well.[59] Climatologists confirm that the Philippines, lying in the western North Pacific, will be experiencing more intense, if not more frequent, tropical cyclones caused by global warming in the coming decades.[60] We can therefore foresee a larger wave of displacement-related migration in the future.

Most migrants are not aware of the external structural factors that drive migration. During the presidency of Corazon Aquino, migrants began to be honored as new heroes (*bagong bayani*). It was a discursive approach, designed to deal with the need to earn more remittances to pay our debts amid the economic crisis left behind by the dictator and to deal with the social costs of migration.[61]

Although remittance flow is a source of high financial benefits, it comes at a formidable social cost, including separation of the family and the vulnerability of migrants to the violation of their human rights (e.g., trafficking, unpaid wages, and sexual violence).

Rhacel Salazar Parreñas observed that Filipinos, when they migrate to work in other countries, become more conscientized

---

[59] "Country Migration Report: The Philippines 2013," https://www.unodc.org/cld/bibliography/2013/country_migration_report_the_philippines_2013.html.

[60] Kerry A. Emanuel, "Downscaling CMIP5 Climate Models Shows Increased Tropical Cyclone Activity over the 21st Century," *PNAS*, 2013, http://www.pnas.org/content/110/30/12219.

[61] Country Migration Report 2013, 99.

and critical about corruption in the home country[62] but feel *utang na loob* toward their host country, oblivious to the latter's possible collaboration in the unequal development of nations that has pushed people to migrate.

Toward Structures of Virtue

Solidarity is the antidote to structures of vice. *Sollicitudo Rei Socialis* defines solidarity as "a firm and persevering determination to commit oneself to the common good; that is to say to the good of all and of each individual because we are all really responsible for all" (no. 38). It is the means to strengthen or create virtuous structures or social structures that steadily foster the human good and human happiness. In the lowland Philippine culture, we speak of a debt of human solidarity (*utang na loob*), which in a global level should be expanded to a consciousness of our debt of global solidarity and, in the context of climate change driving more migration, our debt of earthly solidarity. It is a debt we owe to each other for the very fact of being human and of being co-creatures on this planet.

Advocacy Work

The understanding of how migration can foster development through remittances should not ignore the bigger context of neoliberal global capitalism. It should promote an alternative type of development that fosters self-sufficiency and sustainability. A 2011 study conducted by Carolina González-Velosa, for instance, showed that remittances have been used in a fraction of farms to shift to commercial crops and monocropping, resulting in increased vulnerability to international market prices.[63] Farmers with migrant families should attend

---

[62] See, for example, "Examining the Struggles for Domestic Workers: Hong Kong and the Philippines as Interacting Sites of Activism," *Philippine Political Science Journal* 36, no. 2 (2015): 190–208.

[63] Carolina González-Velosa, "The Effects of Emigration and Remit-

first to the self-sufficiency of their family and village and resort to commercialization only after this need has been addressed. Migrants also need to be aware of the root causes of forced migration, and they should be encouraged to invest in alternative businesses and farming practices. Certain migrants groups have been engaged in migrant conscientization, such as the Mission for Migrant Workers and the Asian Migrant Centre, groups that the church helped organize in the 1980s in Hong Kong. They partner with NGOs that work closely with party-list representatives in the Philippine Congress, who can advance their cause.[64]

Financial Literacy, Livelihood, and Economic Reintegration Programs

The government, the private sector, and civil society have been educating migrants on financial literacy to generate savings, promote investments, and productively use remittances. To help families of OCWs lessen their dependency on remittance, the Catholic Bishops Conference of the Philippines and the Episcopal Commission for the Pastoral Care for Migrants and Itinerant People launched the Diocesan Awareness Seminar for Migrants Apostolate in the islands of Luzon and Mindanao.[65] These seminars, in collaboration with the government's Technical Education and Skills Development Authority, aim to provide skills training to relatives of OCWs to supplement

---

tances on Agriculture: Evidence from the Philippines," 2011, ftp://ftp. cemfi.es/pdf/papers/wshop/JMP_Gonzalezvelosa_JAN.pdf.

[64] The 1987 Philippine Constitution allocates 20 percent of representatives in Congress to party-list groups that come from community sectors or groups that are underrepresented, such as women, labor, and so on. Mission's partner NGO put up the Migrante Sectoral Partylist to represent the concerns of migrants in Congress.

[65] Catholic Bishops Conference of the Philippines, "CBCP Launches Program for OFW Families," September 3, 2014, http://www.cbcpnews. com/cbcpnews/?p=40679.

the income from the migrant and thus further improve their lives. The bishops of Mindanao also recommended the establishment of a Ministry for Migrants in each Mindanao diocese. The Asian Migrant Centre had also organized Unlad Kabayan, an NGO that aims to promote economic reintegration programs for returning migrants. It provides assistance in job hunting and business start-up planning.[66]

In one Catholic migrant parish in Taiwan that welcomes around 700 migrant workers every Sunday, the church uses homilies to educate migrants. The key messages in the homilies include advice about maximizing the benefits of their work experience for the future by paying immediately their loans for placement fees, saving part of their salary (especially overtime pay) for investment in livelihood opportunities, and learning and mastering job skills.[67]

Entrepreneurs likewise come up with creative innovations to prevent hard-earned funds intended for house construction or tuition fees from being diverted toward gambling and extramarital affairs. Cora Tellez, a Filipina entrepreneur in the United States, set up the Gift of Learning and Gift of Health programs (a.k.a. "Regalo"), which guarantee that a remittance is used for its intended purpose. It directs the donor to identify a recipient in the Philippines and to specify the amount to be sent or the schedule of fund remittance, and helps ensure that the donor receives receipts confirming that the money was indeed spent for the intended purpose.

Remittance is a way by which migrants express their *utang na loob* (debt of solidarity) not only to their families and coun-

[66] Graziano Battistella, "Return Migration in the Philippines: Issues and Policies," *International Migration: Prospects and Policies in a Global Marker*, ed. Douglas S. Massey and J. Edward Taylor, Oxford Scholarship Online, 2004, 212–29.

[67] Raymond Calbay, "Homilies as Knowledge Transfer Platform for Filipino Migrant Workers in Taiwan," *Intercultural Communication Studies* 21, no. 3 (2012): 23.

try of origin, but also to their host country. This expression of solidarity can be grounded in a theology of gift where the whole of creation is considered as God's gift (*kaloob*), hence, our obligation to honor our *utang na loob* (debt of solidarity) to our co-creatures. I have discussed how, as such, *utang na loob* can be considered a virtue. *Utang na loob* as a virtue is linked to other virtues such as sacrifice, prudence, and self-care. Its correlative vice is shamelessness (lack of *utang na loob*), which is considered within Philippine culture to be a serious deficiency in character. Stinginess, prodigality, and dependency are other related vices.

The neoliberal capitalist system is a root structure of vice that has led to underdevelopment, driven forced migration, and torn families apart. Solidarity is the antidote to this structure of vice, and I have highlighted some solidarity initiatives of churches toward creating virtuous structures. The challenge is for Philippine migrants to expand their understanding of the virtue of *utang na loob* (debt of solidarity) beyond the familial and communal to include global and even planetary levels.

CHAPTER SIX

Facebook and Populism: Reflections on Cyberethics

There has been a great deal of concern about the role of Facebook in Brexit and in the 2016 US presidential election that led to the victory of Donald Trump. In the 2016 Philippine presidential election that resulted in the victory of President Rodrigo Duterte, an exit poll involving over 45,000 voters revealed that more millennials aged 18–35 voted for him.[1] This is roughly the same age group that uses Facebook the most. As in the United States, however, it is difficult to ascertain to what extent Facebook swayed voters' opinions. When the 2016 Philippine presidential election was held, there were around 30 million users of Facebook in the country,[2] constituting one of the highest Facebook populations in the world.[3]

---

[1] Fleire Castro, "Social Media and Digital Stats in the Philippines 2016 (We Are Social Data)," 2016 http://fleirecastro.com/guides/social-media-and-digital-stats-in-the-philippines-2016-wearesocial-data/.

[2] "Number of Facebook Users in the Philippines from 2015 to 2022 (in Millions)," https://www.statista.com/statistics/490455/number-of-philippines-facebook-users/. Social media refers to Web 2.0 applications that permit content creation and exchange.

[3] This is according to an article on the social news network Rappler titled "A Profile of Internet Users in the Philippines," http://www.rappler.com/brandrap/profile-internet-users-ph. Those who do not have personal computers can access Facebook for free in internet cafes or on their smartphones.

This chapter, which aims to explore possible links between Facebook and populism, will reflect on such potential connections in light of Catholic Church teachings on social communications, with the hope of coming up with a modest guide for cyberethics in an age of populism. The first and second sections of the chapter examine key features of populism, ask if Duterte can qualify as a populist, and explore whether populism is a threat to democracy. The third section delves into how Facebook and its web 2.0 technology has enabled populism. The final section focuses on cyberethics in an age of populism. It gleans guidelines from church teachings that can speak to the distinct role Facebook plays in the spread of populist tactics and reconstructs *hiya* (shame positively construed as sensitivity to the face of the other) as an important vernacular virtue.

Duterte— A Populist? Key Features of Populism

In a literature review that covers the nineteenth to the twenty-first century, Noam Gidron and Bart Bonikowski from Harvard University identified three key features of populism—populism as a thin ideology, as a discursive style, and as a political strategy.[4]

Populism as a Thin Ideology

Based on a study of populist parties in Europe in 2004, political scientist Cas Mudde described populism as a "thin centered ideology" that polarizes society between the "pure

---

[4] Noam Gidron and Bart Bonikowski, "Varieties of Populism: Literature Review and Research Agenda," Weatherhead Center for International Affairs, Harvard University, Working Papers Series, 2014, https://scholar. harvard.edu/files/gidron_bonikowski_populismlitreview_2013.pdf.

people versus the corrupt elite."[5] The ideology is thin because it can be left wing, right wing, or both. It can be linked to all kinds of thick ideologies such as "socialism, nationalism, anti-imperialism or racism, in order to explain the world and justify specific agendas."[6] A key component in the rise of populism is the view that representative democracy has failed the people, that it is a false democracy run by elites who use it to further their own interests. Populism upholds the primacy of the people's will and is different from pluralism, which recognizes the legitimacy of various groups.[7]

Though Duterte has presented himself as a revolutionary, it is not clear what kind of order would replace the system he plans to change. On one hand, he had initially appointed supporters of the Communist Party of the Philippines as heads of the cabinet for social welfare, agrarian reform, and the National Anti-Poverty Commission.[8] On the other hand, he has a propensity toward a dictatorial style of leadership as manifested in his admiration of the late President Ferdinand Marcos, and he prefers the use of state violence over socioeconomic reforms as a means for combating criminality and illegal drugs.

Duterte's enemies are the "yellow armies," who were identified with the elitist democracy of the previous administration and drug dealers and drug addicts, particularly shabu users.[9] He ran on the image of a "crusader from the periphery"—the South of the Philippines—casting his opponents as coming from the oligarchy and political elite class, and thus unconcerned about

---

[5] Cas Mudde, "The Populist Zeitgeist," *Government and Opposition* 39, no. 4 (Autumn 2004): 543–44.

[6] "What Is Populism?" *Economist*, 2016, http://www.economist.com/blogs/economist-explains/2016/12/economist-explains-18.

[7] Mudde, "Populist Zeitgeist."

[8] Two of these nominees failed to pass the approval of the Commission on Appointment and have been replaced.

[9] Similarly, Donald Trump has his own list of enemies: Muslims, illegal immigrants, and the political establishment.

the problems ordinary people face. For example, he lambasted the previous administration for allegedly ignoring the country's drug problem.

Populists also portray traditional media as insincere and thus group journalists with the uncaring elites. This rejection of mass media is an important characteristic of populism on the internet. Duterte supporters hold that the large following (allegedly 4 million) of Mocha Uson—a starlet who became a citizen journalist—is a rejection of traditional media and academic "experts" who are simply "yellow" stooges.[10]

His other enemy are the drug addicts, whom he refers to as "the living walking dead" and who are of "no use to society anymore." Duterte declared that radical action is needed to rein in the drug use that will otherwise destroy the country.[11]

Populism as a Discursive Style

Whereas the first feature of populism focuses on content, the second feature of populism centers on rhetorical style. Based on a study of populism in Latin America, Carlos de la Torre defined populism as a "rhetoric that constructs politics as the moral and ethical struggle between el pueblo [the people] and the oligarchy."[12] Both populism as thin ideology and

---

[10] Carmel Veloso Abao, "The Curious Case of the Mocha Uson Blog," *Rappler*, 2016, http://www.rappler.com/thought-leaders/151250-curious-case-mocha-uson-blog.

[11] Marichu A. Villanueva, "Duterte Likens Drug Addicts to Zombies," *Philippine Star,* August 24, 2016, https://www.philstar.com/opinion/2016/08/24/1616655/duterte-likens-drug-addicts-zombies. According to Duterte, 40 percent of barangay (village) leaders are involved in the trade of illegal drugs. "Expect More Deaths in Renewed Anti-Drug Campaign—Duterte," *Iloilo Metropolitan Times*, March 3, 2017, http://www.iloilometropolitantimes.com/expect-more-deaths-in-renewed-anti-drug-campaign-duterte/.

[12] Carlos de la Torre, *Populist Seduction in Latin America: The Ecuadorian Experience*, Ohio IRS Latin American Series (Athens: Ohio University Press, 2000), 4.

rhetoric emphasize an anti-elite stance and the polarization between "ordinary" people and the elite. But since populist leaders claim to be able to restore power to the common people, it is advantageous if they also use the rhetoric or language of the people.[13] Duterte's rhetorical strategy employs this language or street lingo, even though he hails from a buena familia, that is, an established political family in the South. The masses can identify with his cursing and sexist jokes that are unconstrained by political correctness, his thinking out loud, and his rambling monologues. In a predominantly Catholic country, he cursed Pope Francis, and defended this conduct as his way of "testing the elite in this country."[14]

Populism as a Political Strategy

More common among sociologists and political scientists studying the populist phenomenon in Latin America is the view that populism is a political strategy that centers on policy choices, political organization, and forms of mobilization. For example, populist policies with anti-establishment appeals may aim at the redistribution of wealth, nationalization, and populist mobilization.[15]

Other scholars focus on the political organization of populist parties and regimes. As political scientist Kurt Weyland notes, populism is a strategy in politics whereby a charismatic

---

[13] Teun Pauwels, "Measuring Populism: A Quantitative Text Analysis of Party Literature in Belgium," *Journal of Elections, Public Opinion and Parties* 21, no. 1 (2011): 97–119. Like Duterte, Donald Trump is aware of the importance of brevity (as in a Twitter post), bombastic language, and rash promises.

[14] "Duterte: I Am Testing the Elite in this Country," *Update Philippines*, April 25, 2016, https://www.update.ph/2016/04/duterte-i-am-testing-the-elite-in-this-country/4676.

[15] Raul L. Madrid, "The Rise of Ethnopopulism in Latin America," *World Politics* 60, no. 3 (2008): 482.

leader "seeks or exercises government power based on direct, unmediated, uninstitutionalized support from large numbers of mostly unorganized followers."[16] What is crucial here is the relationship of the leader to the constituents. Though studies of populism frequently refer to the charismatic personality of political leaders, there are cases of noncharismatic populist leaders such as Peru's Alberto Fujimori.[17] Though he was not charismatic, Fujimori projected himself as a strong leader, an "authoritarian strongman."[18] A strong leadership is necessary for representing the will of the people and for bypassing intermediary institutions that may thwart these interests.

Duterte likewise represents himself as a strong leader. One of the top five most popular posts Duterte has made on Facebook states: "I will provide strong leadership to end this country's disorder" (March 20, 2016). And as a populist political strategist, Duterte's policy choices initially included dialogue with the Communist Party of the Philippines and the Moro National Liberation Front—groups that felt excluded in the previous regime's peace talks.

In terms of political organization, Duterte makes sure that those who criticize him are penalized. He had Senator Leila de Lima jailed for leading the investigation on extrajudicial killings. Four senators were ousted from chairmanships in the Senate for attending a rally in EDSA, the site of the two previous people power revolutions in the Philippines, and for speaking against the extrajudicial killings under Duterte.[19]

---

[16] Kurt Weyland, "Clarifying a Contested Concept: Populism in the Study of Latin American Politics," *Comparative Politics* 34, no. 1 (2001): 14.

[17] Robert R. Barr, "Populist, Outsiders, and Anti-establishment Politics," *Party Politics* 15, no. 1 (2009): 29–48.

[18] Indeed, Fujimori supporters believe that he saved Peru from economic devastation and terrorism.

[19] Patricia Lourdes Viray, "LP Senators Ousted from Majority, Committee Posts," *Philippine Star*, February 27, 2017, https://www.philstar.com/headlines/2017/02/27/1675512/lp-senators-ousted-majority-com-

Populism as a Threat to Democracy?

Is populism a threat to democracy? Why should we be concerned about populism? In Europe, the view of populism is negative because of its experience of "populist totalitarian politics," such as those of Adolf Hitler. However, those who studied left-wing populism in Latin America have pointed out that populism can be inclusionary by expanding the democratic participation of groups that have previously been excluded. Benjamin Arditi suggested imagining populism as the specter of democracy, as something that haunts democracy—as a democracy for the elite, because only middle- and upper-class voices are truly represented.[20] He likened populism to "the awkward dinner guest"—"the one who gets drunk and asks inappropriate questions, which may in fact point to important hidden problems."[21] This provocative metaphor illustrates how populism can challenge traditional liberal democracy by highlighting overlooked political problems and give marginalized groups a legitimate voice.[22]

Although populist leaders give primacy to the majority will, this oftentimes come at the cost of bypassing institutional

mittee-posts. Although not all populists are charismatic, Duterte himself is considered charismatic by the poor who identify with his cussing, his sexism, etc.

[20] Benjamin Arditi, *Politics on the Edges of Liberalism: Difference, Populism, Revolution, Agitation* (Edinburgh: Edinburgh University Press, 2007).

[21] B. Moffitt, "Guess Who's Coming to Dinner? Populism as the Awkward Dinner Guest of Democracy," *Connected Globe, Conflicting Worlds*, Australian Political Studies Association Conference, University of Melbourne, September 27–29, 2010.

[22] An example is the American Populist Party, which emerged as a response to the economic depression of the late nineteenth century and aimed at economic reform through the participation of otherwise marginalized groups such as farmers, laborers, and activists—it did, however, exclude minorities. Charles Postel, *The Populist Vision* (Oxford: Oxford University Press, 2007).

processes such as deliberation and checks and balances.[23] Populism can have the effect of threatening the separation of powers of the executive branch, the legislature, and the judiciary, thus weakening democratic institutions. Particularly in unconsolidated democracies, this may eventually lead to the development of an authoritarian regime.[24]

Duterte's disregard for due process is manifested in his refusal to allow the justice system to investigate the extrajudicial killings of drug dealers and users that took place during his time in office, his nonrecognition of the Marcos family's plundering of the nation's wealth, his role in the ousting of the chief justice of the Supreme Court in an attempt to take control of the institution, and so on.

Facebook as Enabler of Populism

There has been little research to date on the role of social media in the rise of populist movements and leaders. But according to Sven Engesser of the Institute of Mass Communication and Media Research at the University of Zurich, online platforms and populism are an ideal combination—social media sites such as Facebook and Twitter allow populist leaders to have a direct line to the people; this enables them to take the people's pulse and to convey their message without the mediation of traditional media.[25]

Facebook is different from traditional media such as newspapers, radio, and television in the following ways: First, it

---

[23] Takis S. Pappas, "Populist Democracies: Post-Authoritarian Greece and Post-Communist Hungary," *Opposition and Government* 49, no. 1 (2013): 1–23.

[24] Steven Levitsky and Lucan A. Way, *Competitive Authoritarianism: Hybrid Regimes after the Cold War* (Cambridge: Cambridge University Press, 2010).

[25] Sven Engesser, Nicole Ernst, Frank Esser, and Florin Büchel, "Populism and Social Media: How Politicians Spread a Fragmented Ideology," *Information, Communication and Society* 20, no. 8 (2016): 1–18.

has empowered the ordinary person to spread a message. The technology allows users to "like" and share a post, thus indicating the popularity of a post. Traditional media outlets often get their news from what is trending on Twitter or Facebook. Online news spills over to traditional media and is spread even to those who have no access to Facebook. Second, it allows for interaction and the possibility to engage in conversation or debate. Whereas in the Web 1.0 era, communication was unilateral because of its "read-only" content, the Web 2.0 discourse (e.g., Facebook and blogs) is more interactive and dynamic. A third feature of the digital interaction allowed by Facebook is its nonhierarchical character. There is no longer a binarism or a distinct division between those who communicate and those who listen. In privileging free peer-to-peer conversations, and allowing for feedback, the digital space offers the possibility of decentering established authorities or institutions.[26]

Facebook also has other features that particularly enable the polarizing approach of populism. First, a person can open multiple accounts under fake names or steal existing accounts. The combination of visual anonymity, mobility, and the virtual nature of computer-mediated communication makes it difficult to know the authenticity of the person one is interacting with. The anonymity and invisibility can lead to toxic disinhibition[27]

---

[26] However, Pauline Hope Cheong has cautioned that although the web has fostered the emergence of new online religious authorities (including women), established leaders or institutions such as the Catholic Church may still maintain unilateral power by disenabling interactive features and thus lessening the possibility of comments and feedback. Pauline Hope Cheong, "From Cyberchurch to Faith Apps: Religion 2.0 on the Rise?" in *Feminist Cyberethics in Asia: Religious Discourses on Human Connectivity*, ed. Agnes M. Brazal and Kochurani Abraham (New York: Palgrave Macmillan, 2014).

[27] See the study of John Suler, the father of cyberpsychology, who identified dissociative anonymity and invisibility as two of six ingredients that enable either benign or toxic disinhibition. John Suler, "The

that reinforces harassment, threats, and other acts of violence on the internet. People feel freer to say things they might never say publicly since it is difficult to police these activities. Second, Facebook enables not only increasing polarization but also the dissemination of fake news by not sufficiently policing professional trolls. The primary agents of fake news in Facebook are the trolls who normally use a fake account so they can easily get away with posting fake news. They are deliberately provocative in their posts to elicit maximum argumentation, or to pick a fight with someone who holds an opposing view.

A study conducted by Facebook involving 700,000 subjects concluded that "when positive expressions were reduced, people produced fewer positive posts and more negative posts; when negative expressions were reduced, the opposite pattern occurred. These results indicate that emotions expressed by others on Facebook influence our own emotions, constituting experimental evidence for massive-scale contagion via social networks."[28] Based on this, therefore, the proliferation of trolls on Facebook can highly polarize its users.

Professional trolls in the Philippines work for legitimate public relations outfits whose job is to manage their clients' social media campaigns. They do this for the money, not necessarily because they believe in the candidate they are promoting online. In the Philippines, profit for such services can reach P100,000 pesos or roughly $2,000 per month.[29]

Online Disinhibition Effect," *Cyberpsychology and Behavior* 7, no. 3 (2004): 321–25.

[28] Adam D. I. Kramer, Jamie E. Guillory, and Jeffrey T. Hancock, "Experimental Evidence of Massive-scale Emotional Contagion through Social Networks," *PNAS* 111, no. 24 (2014): 8788–90.

[29] A similar thing happened during the 2016 US elections, when it was discovered that more than 100 US politics websites were being run from the Former Yugoslav Republic of Macedonia. Two fake stories from these sites made it to the top ten based on Facebook engagement in the final three months before the election. Teens in a Macedonian village earned

Third, Facebook allows the use of social bots. Social bots are software programs that imitate human users of social media to increase the following and online presence of a politician and his or her advocacies.[30] Not only do trolls use fake accounts, they can also pay to tie these accounts to bots or automation programs that mimic one's ideological inclination by feeding it targeted keywords to like or comment on. It is similar to cloning one's self with a robot that will go on a liking and commenting rampage twenty-four hours a day, seven days a week, till one ceases payment. "Bots," which automatically respond or "like" a post, make it seem that there is a surge of public support for a particular candidate or opinion. Since they are driven by machines, each bot can send a thousand posts per minute. By these means, the internet has become—not only during but even after the elections—a "weapon" to misinform and to silence dissent with personal threats such as rape or death.[31]

Last, Facebook reinforces the polarizing stance of populism in its unintended creation of "filter bubbles"[32] or "echo chambers" that insulate one from other people's experiences or

---

a hefty sum of $3,000 and $5,000 per month. Craig Silverman, "This Analysis Shows How Viral Fake Election News Stories Outperformed Real News on Facebook," 2016, https://www.buzzfeed.com/craigsilverman/viral-fake-election-news-outperformed-real-news-on-facebook?utm_term=.co7qL37xe#.hiN8Y5BW3.

[30] Samuel C. Wooley, "Automating Power: Social Bot Interference in Global Politics," *First Monday* 21, no. 4 (April 2016), http://firstmonday.org/ojs/index.php/fm/article/view/6161/5300.

[31] A few months after the 2016 Philippine elections, the social media supporters of Duterte even came out in what they admitted was a "Trollerati" party. "Pres. Duterte's Social Media Supporters Gathered Together for the First Time in a Trollerati Party," 2017, https://www.philnews.xyz/2017/02/pres-duterte-social-media-supporters-trollerati-party-photos-video.html.

[32] Internet activist Eli Pariser coined this term in his book, *The Filter Bubble: What the Internet Is Hiding from You* (New York: Penguin Press, 2011).

opinions. Filter bubbles result from the personalization of the web, whereby your likes and searches on Facebook or Google, along with your particular location, allow a website algorithm to guess or predict the information you would like to see. This can result in the user being isolated from other information that is not in line with one's interest or viewpoints, in effect creating a cultural or ideological bubble, or "tunnel vision." This can also happen when one unfriends all those who hold views that are in opposition to one's perspectives.

Bill Gates remarked in 2017, "[Technology such as social media] lets you go off with like-minded people, so you're not mixing and sharing and understanding other points of view. . . . It's turned out to be more of a problem than I, or many others, would have expected."[33] In his 2017 "Building Global Community" manifesto, Facebook CEO Mark Zuckerberg identified filter bubbles as one of their two most talked about concerns in the past year together with information accuracy, a.k.a. fake news.[34] As in offline communities, online communities are likewise segregated by class, color, cultural, and political perspectives.

The above features of Facebook enable populism in an unprecedented way. The May 2016 election campaign in the Philippines was incredibly virulent and divisive among friends and families. In a predominantly Christian Asian society in which people generally do not criticize each other openly, profanity and personal attacks on others suddenly became the norm on Facebook posts, especially during the elections and for a few months after. The vice president of the Philippines expressed her sorrow over this in a speech to university stu-

---

[33] Kevin J. Delaney, "Filter Bubbles Are a Serious Problem with News, says Bill Gates," *Quartz* (February 21, 2017), https://qz.com/913114/bill-gates-says-filter-bubbles-are-a-serious-problem-with-news/.

[34] Mark Zuckerberg, "Building Global Community," February 16, 2017, https://www.facebook.com/notes/mark-zuckerberg/building-global-community/10154544292806634/.

dents: "It pains me to observe that mean is in and the home-grown values of service and empathy are out."[35] Filipino sociologist Jayeel Cornelio Serrano noted, "The promise of social media is to democratize public participation. Its curse is the spread of hatred."[36]

Cyberethics in an Age of Populism

What can we glean from Catholic teaching—particularly papal messages during World Communication Days and relevant documents of the Pontifical Council for Social Communications (PCSC)[37]—that we can build on to address the above cyberethics issues? What virtues are necessary in social media use? These are the questions that this section will answer.

As background, it was in the papacy of John Paul II that the big mainframe computer was transformed into the personal computers we are familiar with today. Internet was made commercially accessible, and mobile phones also started to proliferate. People started to access websites, communicate via email, sms, and chat. Benedict XVI's papacy saw the emergence of portable devices such as notebooks, tablets, and smartphones; the internet became much faster with broadband, cable and fiber optics, and wireless fidelity (wifi). Facebook was made public in 2006, later to be joined by Twitter, both of which are among the top social networking sites in the world today. Pope Francis is the pope in the era of populism, fake news in social media, and professional trolls.

---

[35] Vice President Leni Robredo, "Service That Counts," Speech at the 107th Commencement Exercises of the University of the Philippines (UP) College of Medicine, July 24, 2016.

[36] It is concerning that this dynamic in social media continued on even after the elections, which is usually a time to reconcile, build coalitions, and work together for the government to succeed.

[37] In 2016, the Pontifical Council for Social Communications was merged into the Secretariat for Communications.

Although social media sites like Facebook did not yet exist in the previous papacies, it does not mean that the teachings on media use in those periods no longer have relevance for the issues at hand.

The Church's Theology of Communication

The document "Church and Internet" (2002), by the Pontifical Council for Social Communications, describes the church's theology of communication as drawn from the theology of communion of the Trinity—the love among the three persons of the Trinity and their reaching out to communicate with humankind. "The Son is the Word, eternally 'spoken' by the Father; and in and through Jesus Christ, Son and Word made flesh, God communicates himself and his salvation to women and men."[38]

The church, or the Christian community, as image of the Trinitarian communion, is called to witness to this divine communication. Human communication, in biblical terms, has journeyed from its collapse at the Tower of Babel due to mutual incomprehension to the restoration of communication and understanding in the Pentecost through the spirit of Jesus.

"Christ is 'the perfect communicator' [Communio et Progressio 11]—the norm and model of the Church's approach to communication, as well as the content that the Church is obliged to communicate."[39] Through Christ who has dismantled barriers of hostility, we are called to be united in community with one another. The desire for connectivity, for knowing others and making ourselves known, manifested in the popularity of social networks such as Facebook and Twitter, is a

---

[38] Pontifical Council for Social Communications (henceforth PCSC), "The Church and Internet" (2002), no. 3, http://www.vatican.va/roman_curia/pontifical_councils/pccs/documents/rc_pc_pccs_doc_20020228_church-internet_en.html.

[39] Ibid., no. 12.

manifestation of our being "created in the image and likeness of God, the God of communication and communion."[40]

Principles and Norms for the Ethical Evaluation of Social Communication

The Human Person and the Common Good

John Paul II in his "Communications Media at the Service of Understanding Peoples" (2005) identified the human person and the human community as the fundamental ethical principle in the evaluation of communications (no. 21).[41] As earlier expressed by John XXIII in *Pacem in Terris*, this entails promotion of the common good that goes beyond the limited concerns of a particular group or nation, to foster the good of all (no. 132).[42]

Toward the integral development of persons and that of the common good, John Paul II, in "The Communications Media at the Service of Authentic Peace in the Light of *Pacem in Terris*," stressed the duty of media to uphold truth, freedom, justice, and love/solidarity, the same norms that John XXIII identified as necessary to guide various forms of relations (no. 163).[43] Though "Communications Media at the Service of

---

[40] Benedict XVI, "New Technologies, New Relationships: Promoting a Culture of Respect, Dialogue and Friendship," World Communications Day 2009, http://w2.vatican.va/content/benedict-xvi/en/messages/communications/documents/hf_ben-xvi_mes_20090124_43rd-world-communications-day.html.

[41] PCSC, *Ethics in Communications*, 2000 http://www.vatican.va/roman_curia/pontifical_councils/pccs/documents/rc_pc_pccs_doc_20000530_ethics-communications_en.html.

[42] John XXIII, *Pacem in Terris*, 1963, http://w2.vatican.va/content/john-xxiii/en/encyclicals/documents/hf_j-xxiii_enc_11041963_pacem.html.

[43] John Paul II, "The Communications Media at the Service of Authentic Peace in the Light of *Pacem in Terris*" (henceforth "Communications

Authentic Peace" was addressed to media professionals, the principles it identified are fruitful resources for guiding all individuals or groups making use of computer-mediated communication networks, as can be seen in their deployment by later church documents as norms in addressing cyber-communication issues.

Media and Truth

Communication, according to John Paul II, must be in the service of truth. Truth pertains not only to facts or accurate information but also to those relating to the vocation of humans as persons, the common good of society, and our relationship with the Divine.

The document by the PCSC, *Ethics in Communications* (2000), cites instances of how media can be employed to marginalize people, to entice them to be part of "perverse communities organized around false, destructive values; fostering hostility and conflict, demonizing others and creating a mentality of 'us' against 'them'; . . . spreading misinformation and disinformation."[44] *Ethics in Communications* was written before Facebook emerged, but the message applies very well to the dissemination of hate currently propagated by trolls.

Ethics in Communications also speaks of how media is used by politicians to deceive people and "misrepresent opponents and systematically distort and suppress the truth by propaganda and 'spin'" (no. 15). Today, this is done by politicians who employ public relations outfits that in turn make use of trolls and bots to manage their campaigns.

Media") noted that the emerging developments in information and communication technologies form part of the cultural context of *Pacem in Terris*. Since its publication in 1963, developments in media communication have grown exponentially.

[44] PCSC, *Ethics in Communications*, no. 13.

Media and Freedom

John Paul II links freedom to responsibility and to truth. The pope stressed that it is access to true and adequate information that serves freedom and genuine community.[45] He also emphasized the need for the media to operate in an atmosphere of freedom. Though it should be regulated, the pope cautioned that it should not be controlled by the government. *Ethics in Communications* explains that the "presumption should always be in favor of freedom of expression," which is both a right and a duty.[46] However, this is not absolute, as there are cases such as "libel and slander, messages that seek to foster hatred and conflict among individuals and groups, obscenity and pornography, the morbid depiction of violence—where no right to communicate exists."[47] Freedom of expression must always be guided by truth, respect for privacy, and justice.

"The Church and Internet" (2002) adds that "while respect for free expression may require tolerating even voices of hatred up to a point, industry self-regulation—and, where required, intervention by public authority—should establish and enforce reasonable limits to what can be said."[48]

The issue of responsible freedom is also involved in the case of professional or paid trolls. The libertarian roots of the internet in the counterculture of first-generation users, combined with its commercial nature, today have fostered "radical libertarianism or the absolutization of freedom."[49] It is within this cultural milieu that one may view professional trolls whose only concern is to earn money with utter disregard for how their

---

[45] John Paul II, "Communications Media," no. 5.

[46] PCSC, *Ethics in Communications*, no. 23.

[47] Ibid.

[48] PCSC, "The Church and Internet," no. 8.

[49] PCSC, "Ethics in Internet," no. 8, http://www.vatican.va/roman_curia/pontifical_councils/pccs/documents/rc_pc_pccs_doc_20020228_ethics-internet_en.html.

actions affect society. In the anonymity of the internet, trolls can escape from being accountable for their actions. "Ethics in Internet" critiques this radical libertarianism or absolutization of freedom at the expense of truth. Trolls with bots do not even "see" whom they are attacking, as it is the bots that go on a rampage with their hateful comments. Pope Francis's words speak to this: "Access to digital networks entails a responsibility for our neighbour whom we do not see but who is nonetheless real and has a dignity which must be respected."[50] Benedict XVI, in "Children and Media" (2007),[51] encouraged formation in the proper exercise of freedom, which is not simply the pursuit of happiness and novel experiences but the capacity to choose what is true, good, and beautiful.

Media and Justice

John Paul II related media and justice to the universal common good. Justice, according to the pope, can be served by faithfully representing events, and correctly discussing and presenting issues from the perspective of various standpoints.

Today, the facts may be out there, but because we are confined to our echo chambers, we are unable to access the truth. In the 48th World Communications Day message, Pope Francis indirectly refers to this filter bubble that can barricade us from a variety of sources of information and perspectives.[52] How then do we get out of this bubble? Pope Francis

---

[50] Francis, "Communication and Mercy: A Fruitful Encounter," World Communications Day, 2016, https://w2.vatican.va/content/francesco/en/messages/communications/documents/papa-francesco_20160124_messaggio-comunicazioni-sociali.html.

[51] Benedict XVI, "Children and Media: A Challenge for Education," World Communications Day, 2007, https://w2.vatican.va/content/benedict-xvi/en/messages/communications/documents/hf_ben-xvi_mes_20070124_41st-world-communications-day.html.

[52] Francis, "Communication at the Service of an Authentic Culture of Encounter," World Communications Day, 2014, https://w2.vatican.va/

illustrated this through his favorite parable, that of the Good Samaritan, which is also a parable about communication. "It is not just about seeing the other as someone like myself, but of the ability to make myself like the other"[53]—to see things from the perspective of the other. This may mean intentionally looking for these other points of view or even joining these other Facebook groups.

Furthermore, in his 2017 message, referring to the power we now have to share news instantly and spread it widely, the pope encouraged social media users to break the constant focus on bad news that glamorizes evil and instead share solutions and good news that gives hope.[54]

Media and Solidarity

Love or solidarity in *Pacem in Terris* is a caring for the needs of others as if they are one's own, leading toward sharing of goods and mutual collaboration. John Paul II linked this to the role of media in building trust among peoples and nations.[55] "Ethics in Internet," no. 15, speaks of the virtue of solidarity as "the measure of the Internet's service of the common good." New technologies have made it easier for different cultures and religions to dialogue with one another. They can thus be employed to foster friendship and solidarity.[56]

content/francesco/en/messages/communications/documents/papa-francesco_20140124_messaggio-comunicazioni-sociali.html.

[53] Ibid.

[54] Francis, "Fear Not for I Am with You: Communicating Hope and Trust in Our Time," (Is. 43:5)," World Communications Day, 2017, https://w2.vatican.va/content/francesco/en/messages/communications/documents/papa-francesco_20170124_messaggio-comunicazioni-sociali.html.

[55] John Paul II, "Communications Media," no. 6.

[56] Benedict XVI, "New Technologies, New Relationships: Promoting a Culture of Respect, Dialogue and Friendship," World Communications Day, 2009, http://w2.vatican.va/content/benedict-xvi/en/messages/communications/documents/hf_ben-xvi_mes_20090124_43rd-world-communications-day.html.

Speaking specifically to the European Union, Pope Francis cited solidarity as "the most effective antidote" to various types of populism today. Solidarity entails awareness that though we are different, we are parts of one body regardless of nation, ethnicities, and religion, and thus this view should move us to look beyond tribalism and particularisms.[57]

Facebook and the Challenge of the Common Good

The responsibility of the company behind Facebook needs to be examined in relation to how its technological features are promoting the rapid dissemination of fake news and thereby compromising truth, freedom, and justice. As the document "Ethics in Internet" points out, "Those whose decisions and actions contribute to shaping the structure and contents of the Internet have an especially serious duty to practice solidarity in the service of the common good" (no. 15).

In 2017, in response to mounting criticisms, Facebook started moving from defending itself as simply a "platform empowering its users to voice their opinions"[58] to acknowledging its role as a forum for "authentic communication,"[59] and finally decided to address the problem of fake news. The company constructed a model that is able to detect posts that are inauthentic or game feeding (asking for likes, comments, or shares). According to Facebook, this will not entirely elimi-

---

[57] James Carroll, "Pope Francis Proposes a Cure for Populism," March 28, 2017, http://www.newyorker.com/news/news-desk/pope-francis-proposes-a-cure-for-populism.

[58] Jakub Goda, "The Far Right's Facebook Megaphone," *Politico*, December 10, 2016, https://www.politico.eu/article/the-far-rights-facebook-megaphone-populism-facebook/.

[59] Facebook Security, "Making Facebook Safe and Secure for Authentic Communication," April 27, 2017, https://www.facebook.com/notes/facebook-security/making-facebook-safe-and-secure-for-authentic-communication/10154362152760766/.

nate fake news, but such items will appear lower down on the user's feed, depending both on how closely linked you are to the person sharing and on the post's popularity. Another 2017 Facebook initiative was the rolling out of a fake news alert that would introduce warning labels on stories that have been deemed false by fact-checkers. Facebook's 1.7 billion users can flag stories or links they think are fake news, which will then be sent to a small list of fact-checkers who will make a judgment on whether the story is true or not. The fact-checkers are members of the International Fact-Checking Network that espouses nonpartisanship, transparency, and fairness.[60] News reported to be fake will now be "flagged" by Facebook, with an accompanying red label claiming the story is "disputed by 3rd Party Fact-Checkers."[61] A user who wants to share a story that has been labeled as fake news will see a pop-up dialogue box with a caution and a question about whether or not they nevertheless want to share it.

Fake news items and sites are also "powerful drivers of profit."[62] Recently, however, the top two online advertising

---

[60] Bart Cammaerts, "Facebook's Fake News Fact-checking alert will be the Saviour of the Mainstream Media," March 23, 2017, http://www.independent.co.uk/voices/facebook-fake-news-fact-check-google-ad-save-journalism-a7645706.html.

[61] Virginia Hale, "'Fake News' Causing Populism, Must Be Censored, says Italy's Antitrust Chief," December 30, 2016, http://www.breitbart.com/london/2016/12/30/fake-news-must-censored-italy/.

[62] Katherine Haenschen and Paul Ellenbogen illustrated and outlined how the fake news industry produces profits, as follows: "1. An individual publishes false information on a Fake News website, then pays to advertise a link to the post in Facebook users' newsfeeds. 2. Facebook profits from advertising on its platform, earning money for every person who clicks the link or every 1,000 users who see the ads. 3. Facebook users click on the advertised links and go to the Fake News website, generating an impression for each display ad on the website. 4. The Fake News site earns revenue from the resulting advertising impressions, which amount to millions of page views and tens of thousands of dollars per month. 5. Fake News producers advertise their page to fans, growing an organic Facebook audi-

companies, Google and Facebook, banned fake news sites from using their ad services. DoubleVerify, which provides a tool for advertisers to restrict where ads run, released a new filter for fake news websites.[63] For Germany, however, the efforts made by Facebook are not sufficient. In anticipation of the massive use of the internet in the 2017 elections in Germany in September, a bill was passed[64] that imposes a fine of as much as $53 million for Facebook and other social networks if they will not allow users to complain about fake news and hate speech and/or if they refuse to take down flagged illegal content. Referring to a study conducted by his ministry, Justice Minister Heiko Maas said that Twitter deleted only 1 percent and Facebook 39 percent of posts tagged as illegal by users. By comparison Google's YouTube has removed 90 percent of marked illegal posts.[65] The law known as NetzDG went into full effect in January 2018 and requires social networks to remove clearly illegal content within twenty-four hours after it has been tagged, and to remove fake posts within a week. Critics, however, are denouncing this as a violation of the right to freedom of speech.[66]

In 2018, Zuckerberg confirmed, in response to accusations, that there had been a major breach of Facebook accounts

---

ence to whom they can share links at no cost. 6. Fans can share these links to their own Facebook networks, furthering the organic reach of Fake News. This is how something 'goes viral.'" Haenschen and Ellenbogen, "Disrupting the Business Model of the Fake News Industry," *Freedom to Tinker*, December 14, 2016, https://freedom-to-tinker.com/2016/12/14/disrupting-the-business-model-of-the-fake-news-industry/.

[63] Paresh Dave, "Without These Ads, There Wouldn't Be Money in Fake News," *Los Angeles Times*, April 9, 2017, http://www.latimes.com/business/technology/la-fi-tn-fake-news-ad-economy-20161208-story.html.

[64] Stefan Nikola and Birgit Jennen, "Germany Gets Really Serious about Fake News on Facebook," *Bloomberg*, April 5, 2017, https://www.bloomberg.com/news/articles/2017-04-05/merkel-cabinet-backs-facebook-fines-to-stem-fake-news-in-germany.

[65] Ibid.

[66] Ibid.

(now estimated at 87 million users), 50 million of which were used by Cambridge Analytica to develop a powerful software program that can predict how voters will behave, thereby potentially capable as well of influencing the results of an election. This is said by some to have catapulted Donald Trump to the US presidency. Some believe it may also have been employed in the Brexit polls that led to the British vote to leave the European Union. Much earlier than the Brexit vote and Trump's election, the chief social media strategist of Duterte's campaign, who was caught in a photo dining with the CEO of Cambridge Analytica, admitted to being influenced by the latter, but denied having availed himself of their services. As a result of this controversy, Zuckerberg committed to strengthening the privacy settings of Facebook in order to protect user accounts.

Reappropriating the Cardinal Virtues for Social Media Use

"The Church and Internet" and other church documents speak of the cardinal moral virtues (or good habits) that allow for an ethical use of the internet.

Prudence

Aristotle taught us that prudence is "right reason applied to practice." Parents, John Paul II admonished in 1981 in *Familiaris Consortio*, should train children in the "moderate, critical, watchful and prudent use of the media" (no. 76). The PCSC's "Ethics in Internet" also notes that educational institutions should enable both children and adults to be "discerning" in their use of internet content (no. 15). As a concrete example of this, Facebook users should be taught how to distinguish between valid and fake sources of news, as well as between real humans and social bots. A social bot normally has no picture and contains very little or no information at all about the user.

Justice

Justice in "Church and Internet" is aimed at closing the digital divide. This is still necessary in the Philippine context as not everyone has access to the internet. Justice can also take the form of mainstream news websites using the vernacular to provide the masses with access to contemporary news coverage.

In addition, justice is promoted when, for example, lawyers offered their services for free to young women who were slut-shamed by Facebook users because they were demonstrating against the burial—initiated by Duterte—of the late president and dictator Marcos at the Heroes' Cemetery (*Libingan ng mga Bayani*). Those who abuse the right to communicate should indeed be made answerable before the law.

Temperance

"The Church and Internet" notes that temperance is "a self-disciplined approach to . . . the Internet, so as to use it wisely and only for good" (no. 12). This entails thinking before sending; avoiding the temptation to immediately share "memes" that appeal to one's emotions without investigating first the veracity of the content. Better yet, it should be a practice by all to footnote a meme with the reference. Another practice of temperance on Facebook is that of "starving the troll" by ignoring it. Sharing or commenting "feeds the troll" and makes the fake news/post even more popular, and trolls thrive on attention.

One can also link the virtue of temperance to Pope Francis's emphasis on the need "to recover a certain sense of deliberateness and calm. This calls for time and the ability to be silent and to listen."[67]

---

[67] Francis, Message for the 48th World Communications Day: Communication at the Service of an Authentic Culture of Encounter, Sunday, 1 June 2014.

Fortitude

Fortitude, or courage, is necessary for decency in the face of vitriolic attacks on the internet. People have received rape or death threats for expressing opposing views on Facebook. Fortitude can be expressed in the form of feedback or a friendly correction to those who propagate hate messages and fake news.

Recovering/Reinventing Hiya (Shame) as Virtue

I have emphasized earlier the importance of recovering vernacular virtues that may have been ignored or even vilified in the period of colonial Christianity and civilization. Shame is among these virtues.

Although most cultures, if not all, have a concept of shame, it assumes a great importance among honor cultures in Mediterranean societies[68] and among Asians, especially those with strong Chinese influence, including those in Southeast Asia.[69] The Chinese have 113 shame terms with a focus on either the state of shame focused on the self (fear of losing face, feeling after losing face, and guilt) or on reactions to shame in relation to others (disgrace, shamelessness and its denunciation, and embarrassment).

Most Western theorists in the twentieth century have evaluated shame negatively, as an infantile emotion (Erik Erikson), an inhibiting self-expression (gestalt therapy), or as a negative energy to be discharged (bioenergetic therapy). In contrast, guilt is regarded as potentially good and redemptive because it incorporates feelings of responsibility.[70]

---

[68] See, for instance, Bruce J. Malina and Jerome H. Neyrey, "Honor and Shame in Luke-Acts: Pivotal Values of the Mediterranean World," in *The Social World of Luke-Acts: Models for Interpretation*, ed. Jerome Neyrey (Peabody, MA: Hendrickson, 1991), 25–66.

[69] See Jin Li, Lianqin Wang, and Kurt W. Fischer, "The Organisation of Shame Concepts," *Cognition and Emotion* 18, no. 6 (2004): 768.

[70] David W. Augsburger, *Pastoral Counseling across Cultures* (Phila-

Ian MacLeod contrasted shame with guilt. In his view, shame is felt when one is not able to conform to the expectations of others,[71] whereas guilt is the painful feeling when one fails to fulfill one's responsibility. The latter is thus an indication of a superior morality. In *Pastoral Counseling across Cultures*, David Augsburger likewise contrasted shame and guilt.[72] Whereas shame involves losing face "before significant persons," guilt is condemnation or losing integrity "before one's own conscience." Whereas shame is embarrassment before social expectations, guilt is pain before moral standards. Shame leads to discretion, whereas guilt leads to integrity. Shame urges one to recover face and regain honor, whereas guilt pushes one to repent and act responsibly.[73]

The negative view of shame has been challenged recently, and an alternative perspective has been proposed by psychologists and philosophers who have highlighted shame as a "self-conscious moral emotion" and virtue, especially in non-Western societies.

In Confucianism, shame is both a moral feeling and a capacity to examine one's self with the goal of transformation according to social and moral ideals.[74] It is considered a major

---

delphia: Westminster Press, 1986), 114. The distinction between shame and guilt cultures was first pointed out by Ruth Benedict in *The Chrysanthemum and the Sword: Patterns of Japanese Culture*, foreword by Ian Buruma, Mariner book edition (1964; Boston: Houghton Mifflin, 2005).

[71] It thus blocks a genuine disclosure of the self. In a paper given by MacLeod in a Missionary Seminar in 1982, he notes: "Shame always stands between people and pushes them apart. It never draws people together. It makes for concealment, not disclosure of self. It leads to lies, anger and avoidance. . . . It is the mark of a slavery to the opinions and attitudes of others, not of autonomy and inwardly responsibly-formed value judgments. . . . Pride and its reverse side shame is the original sin." Ian MacLeod, "The Dynamics of Shame and Guilt," in *Can the Gospel Thrive in Japanese Soil?* (Tokyo: Hayama Missionary Seminar, 1982).

[72] Augsburger, *Pastoral Counseling across Cultures*, 122.

[73] Ibid.

[74] Heidi Fung, "Affect and Early Moral Socialization: Some Insights

virtue, an ability that should be possessed by scholar officials (Analects 13.20), and it is one of the four foundations of a good moral disposition (Mencius 2A6, 6A6). The ideal person in early Confucian philosophy is marked by a sense of shame. Though shame is strongly felt in front of others, in the Confucian perspective it is more of a reflexive awareness of failing to live up to one's moral ideal, and is driven by a desire for moral growth. In early Confucian philosophy, there is no sense that shame can be harmful to a person. In fact, a person without a sense of shame is considered to be "beyond moral reach." Shame is more than just a positive ideal; it is a virtuous sensibility that needs to be nurtured.[75]

Discourses on Hiya

The Confucian concept of shame is similar to the Filipino concept of *hiya*, a term used to refer to shame as both guilt and embarrassment. Post–World War II psychologists and socio-anthropologists in the Philippines likewise viewed hiya as something negative. They translated it into English as shame, embarrassment, shyness, timidity, and bashfulness, resulting from an "unindividuated ego" and thus an "inferior form of morality."[76] Because it is said to be motivated purely by the desire to be accepted by society or by the particular person

---

and Contributions from Indigenous Psychological Studies in Taiwan," in *Indigenous and Cultural Psychology: Understanding People in Context*, ed. Uichol Kim, Kuo-Shu Yang, and Kwang-Kuo Hwang (Boston: Springer, 2006), 175–96.

[75] Ibid.

[76] For Jaime Bulatao, *hiya* is "a painful emotion arising from a relationship with an authority figure or with society inhibiting self-assertion in a situation which is perceived as dangerous to one's ego." For him it is a mechanism that protects the "unindividuated ego." "Hiya," *Philippine Studies Journal* 12 (January 1964): 424, 428, 435.

involved, hiya reinforces social conformity[77] and thus can trap people in a conspiracy of silence. However, the weakness of the above readings lies in their heavy reliance on English categories and concepts[78] and the primacy given to individual moral autonomy over relationality. Thus the local concept (hiya) was made to fit into a particular Western view of shame.

Also absent from the above writings are the socio-economic-political contexts in which hiya arises. Michael Pinches pointed out how the poor oftentimes feel shame not only for their condition of poverty but also for being unable to express their discontent in the face of an authoritarian employer for fear of losing their job.[79] He also noted how hiya has often been invoked in the context of *utang na loob* (debt of gratitude), particularly in patronage politics. Politicians demand debt of gratitude for providing material gifts and services (which is supposed to be part of their job) and sanction with shame those who do not comply.

Hiya involves not only an external dimension (embarrassment before others) but an internal dimension as well, as with the Chinese concept of shame.[80] Filipinos have the saying,

---

[77] For the sociologist Frank Lynch, the main motivation underlying hiya is the need to be accepted by society. "Social Acceptance Reconsidered," in *Four Readings in Philippine Values*, ed. Frank Lynch and Alfonso de Guzman II (Metro-Manila: Ateneo de Manila University Press, 1970), 16.

[78] Virgilio Enriquez, "Is Filipino Psychology Endangered by the English Language?" in *New Directions in Indigenous Psychology*, ed. Allen Aganon and S. Ma. Assumpta David, RVM (Manila: National Book Store, 1985), 70.

[79] Michael Pinches, "The Working-Class Experience of Shame, Inequality, and People Power in Tatalon, Manila," in *From Marcos to Aquino: Local Perspectives on Political Transition in the Philippines*, ed. Benedict J. Kerkvliet and Resil B. Mojares (Honolulu: University of Hawai'i Press, 1991), 179.

[80] This should be understood within a concept of self where the *loob* (inside) is integrally related to the *labas* (outside) and the boundaries between the external and the internal are blurred. For a critique of those who represent shame in early Confucianism as solely involving the inter-

"*Nahiya sa ibang tao, pero hindi nahiya sa Diyos*." (He or she felt shame before others but not before God.) A feeling of shame before God is more commonly associated with guilt. *Nahihiya ako* (I feel shame) is sometimes used interchangeably with "My conscience is bothering me." It leads to acting responsibly. To have shame is to fulfill one's duty as a father or a mother. In this sense, hiya can also be described as sensitivity to a possible loss of one's face or the face of the other.

Filipino philosopher Jeremiah Reyes further distinguished two meanings of hiya in terms of: (1) the *hiya* that is suffered (a passion), akin to embarrassment or shyness, and (2) the *hiya* that stems from an "active and sacrificial self-control" (a virtue).[81] These two are not mutually exclusive, however, and can both be present in a particular incident.

In making this distinction, Reyes was influenced by Thomas Aquinas who differentiated between shame (*verecundia*) and temperance (*temperantia*). Verecundia is fear of public shame.[82] This fear restrains a person from doing something reprehensible or causes the feeling of shame for what one is doing. Temperantia is a cardinal virtue that is the habit of self-restraint in the area of the individual bodily appetites such as sex, food, and drink.[83]

Reyes associated hiya with the virtue of temperance; it allows a person to control himself or herself from acting inconsiderately, or from exploiting a generous offer. The nearest word to hiya as temperance is *kahihiyan* or a sense of propriety or *delicadeza*. It restrains one from insulting others, especially in public, because of concern or compassion for the face of the other. Both temperance and hiya restrain. But while temperance controls natural appetite for food, drink,

---

nal dimension, see Jane Geaney, "Guarding Moral Boundaries: Shame in Early Confucianism," *Philosophy East and West* 54, no. 2 (2004): 113–42.

[81] Jeremiah Reyes, "In Defense of Hiya as a Virtue," *Asian Philosophy* 26, no. 1 (2016): 66–78.

[82] *Summa Theologiae* II–II, q. 144, a. 2.

[83] *Summa Theologiae* I–II, q. 66, a. 4.

and sex, hiya restrains in relation to the social and relational dimension. And while temperance can be exercised as a solitary individual, hiya is integrally relational, that is, exercised only in relation with other people.

Lack of hiya is thus a moral deficiency and its possession a moral obligation. A person without hiya is called thick-faced (*makapal ang mukha*). Shame is automatically connected to the face. The concrete face expresses shame literally (as in blushing or the hiding of one's face), as well as metaphorically. We speak of a loss of face when one loses honor and respect. In the Philippines, we say "*walang mukhang ihaharap*" or "no face to show" when one has done something shameful.

Face in Philippine anthropology is thus more than just a front we put on for each other; the face is a mirror or a reflection of one's inner self (loob),[84] character, or dignity.[85] It is important to have a (good) face to show before society. To lose face is to feel humiliatingly exposed, in one's lack of integrity or respect, in one's meanness or weakness, not only before others but also in front of one's inner self (ego ideal or conscience) as well as before God. It is not uncommon to see on national television people who have committed crimes demonstrating some sense of shame (hiya), literally hiding or covering their faces to conceal their identities. Losing face on the part of the victimizer seems a necessary phase toward regaining one's dignity as a person. Transcending the shame-guilt dichotomy, hiya is concerned not only with the "loss of face before significant others" but also with the "loss of integrity before one's own conscience." Hiya is ultimately linked with preserving dignity that is not simply ascribed by other humans but God-given.

---

[84] It is, however, possible to hide what is within and to show a different face. From a postmodern perspective, all of these faces are parts of one's multiple selves. See Suler, "The Online Disinhibition Effect," 324–25.

[85] This was noted by Pinches in his fieldwork in Tatalon. Pinches, "Working-Class Experience of Shame," 308n16.

As with the Chinese, it is a great insult to be called shameless or "walang hiya," oftentimes used to refer to people who exploit others, who are insensitive to the effects of their actions on others. The two pillars of hiya are the inner self (loob) and the "other" (kapwa). It is only in relation to these two concepts, Reyes argues, that one can classify hiya as a virtue. "A person without hiya is also one whose loob [heart] is hard as rock . . . and therefore has no damay [compassion or caring]. A situation is kahiya-hiya [shameful] when an individual fails to respond to or deliberately ignores the 'other' who shows him love, caring, or simply hospitality."[86] Hiya suggests a person's sensitivity (pakiramdam) to the way she or he relates with others. This underlies expressions such as *may kahihiyan* (has a sense of shame), *marunong mahiya* (knows how to feel shame), and *hindi marunong mahiya* (unable to feel shame). As a "painful emotion," it is a barometer of the violation of a person's dignity. Ferdinand Dagmang noted that those who are able to feel shame have greater sensitivity to the need for help and caring of those who have lost their face in society.[87]

Such a caring attitude does not just concern interpersonal relations but is a mark of ideal citizenship as well. Andres Bonifacio, one of the Philippine national heroes who fought against the Spanish and US American colonizers, noted that what was needed in the revolutionary group Katipunan was someone who loved the country and possessed hiya because only such a person could offer his life for the country.[88] A Philippine revolutionary Constitution written in 1902 during the period of American colonization prescribed the need for

---

[86] Reynaldo Clemeña Ileto, *Pasyon and Revolution: Popular Movements in the Philippines, 1840–1910* (Metro-Manila: Ateneo de Manila University Press, 1979), 157–58.

[87] Ferdinand Dagmang, "Hiya: Daan at Kakayahan sa Pakikipag-kapwa," *MST Review* 1, no. 1 (1996): 66–90.

[88] Ileto, *Pasyon and Revolution*, 158.

all to have "hiya and purity of self, so that mutual caring shall not be lost."[89] The Katipunan code of conduct teaches: "To the person who has hiya, his/her word is an oath." Hiya in this context is associated with being true to one's word, the correspondence between what one says and does, or the integration of one's personal and inner self or loob. These are more fully captured by the terms *truthfulness, fidelity, honesty,* and *integrity,* which are necessary to maintain harmony not only within one's self, but within the collective self as well (one's family and society).

This is similar to the Chinese concept of shame, where shame can be shared by a collectivity (Analects 2.3) or even a country (Mencius 4A7). Far from being a sign of an unindividuated ego,[90] hiya is a mark of a truly autonomous self-in-relation and is important for attaining unity and social harmony.

Hiya in the Scriptures

The Scriptures speak of shame as timidity or embarrassment, and emphasize that neither the gospel (2 Tim 1:8; Rom 1:16) nor the suffering because one is a Christian (2 Tim 1:8; Mark 8:38; 1 Peter 4:16) is a cause for timidity or embarrassment. But it likewise speaks of a shame that is a moral good: the shame one feels when one sins (1 Cor 15:24; 1 Cor 6:5; Ez 43:10).

The story of Adam and Eve (Gen 3:1–21) illustrates shame as a painful emotion resulting from an awareness of one's failure to meet a moral ideal. When Adam and Eve heard God walking in the garden, they wanted to hide and cover themselves. God called them out and helped them to gradually admit what they had done. Indeed, they had to suffer the consequences of their actions—the loss of face before all of creation, the departure from paradise and its life of comfort.

---

[89] Ibid., 181.
[90] Dagmang, "Hiya," 70–73, 88.

However, God also enfaced them. Genesis 3:21 says, "And the LORD God made garments of skins for the man and for his wife, and clothed them." God covered their shame with divine clothing. In Revelation 3:5, Jesus says, "The one who conquers will be *clothed* in *white garments*, and I will never blot his *name* out of the book of life. I will *confess his name* before my Father and before his angels." Being clothed with divine garments thereby suggests restoration of one's name as acceptable before God.

Shame (Hiya) as Virtue in the Context of Cyber-Interaction

Trolls (paid or not) and those who propagate fake news have lost kahihiyan or their sense of propriety. Many have accepted payment in exchange for promoting a candidate by trolling. On the one hand, there is the individualist orientation that is focused only on earning or profit and not the common good. On the other hand, it is the situation of anonymity, invisibility, or facelessness due to the use of fake accounts that removes the sanction of shame. In this context, the concept of hiya as inner compass truly needs to be recovered. Teaching students to see hiya as a virtue can be a step forward.

The virtue of hiya as a capacity for restraint in the face of offensive messages is also called for in the case of victims of trolls' curse words, personal attacks, and slut-shaming. Enfacement or vindication should be mediated via a community. In *The Female Face of God in Auschwitz*, Melissa Raphael showed that redeeming the face, the overcoming of shame, is mediated primarily through the community.[91] As Steven Pattison expressed it, "If God's people are defiled, then God's image cannot be seen—the people cannot see God. But equally,

---

[91] Melissa Raphael, *The Female Face of God in Auschwitz: A Jewish Feminist Theology of the Holocaust* (London: Routledge, 2003).

God cannot see Godself reflected in Israel."[92] This notion of a mutual dependence of humans and God in revealing each other's faces is, as Pattison noted, more common in Jewish theology. It is, however, important for Christianity as well. Humans co-participate with God in rendering visible the face of God. In lay terms, a community must make visible the face of God, otherwise "God has no face on earth."[93]

In the cyber-context, this implies that the redeeming of faces is not just an individual task but also a community and social endeavor. Collective efforts to identify and sue the perpetrators can serve to enface the victim-survivors. Shaming for the common good can be a way to shake the purveyors of fake news and trolls from their complacency. We have noted earlier how conscientious Philippine netizens, in an effort to enface the victims, sought to expose the real identities of slut-shamers while a group of lawyers offered free legal aid to victims of slut-shaming. This is in continuity with practices in the Philippines and other parts of Asia such as China, where "shaming" or exposing the face of the victimizers or violators of the law has been practiced with some success. Such shaming is regarded as ultimately for the good of the person and as a means to prevent him or her from doing the same thing in the future. It is likewise a form of enfacing, of redeeming the face of the perpetrator.

Political leaders and citizens should be affirmed as well for possessing the virtue of "hiya" (being true to one's word, possessing a sense of integrity), instead of being applauded for catering simply to what is "popular."

Populism and online platforms such as Facebook are a potent combination. Social media sites have enabled populist leaders to communicate with the people they are representing without the mediation of traditional media.

---

[92] Stephen Pattison, *Saving Face: Enfacement, Shame, Theology*, Kindle ed. (London: Routledge, 2014), 141.

[93] Raphael, *The Female Face of God in Auschwitz*, 154.

Separately considered, populism and certain features of Facebook can threaten democracy. Populism becomes a threat to democracy when it sidesteps the separation of powers and institutional processes in order to respond to the "will of the people." Facebook threatens democratic discussion and deliberation when it does not seriously censure: (1) the creation of fake news through trolls; (2) the rapid dissemination of fake news through social bots; and (3) the polarization of discussions through the flaming tactics of trolls, which is further reinforced by the filter bubbles that insulate users from opposing viewpoints. With these features, Facebook has enabled populist tactics of polarization in unprecedented ways.

The Catholic Church, through the Papal Messages for World Communications Day and documents released by the Pontifical Council for Social Communications, has provided basic principles, norms, and virtues that we can build on to address the above issues. In the Philippine context, a vernacular virtue, hiya, also needs to be recovered and strengthened and used to sanction fake news purveyors, trolls, and politicians that employ them. Both the users and creators of Facebook are enjoined to promote the universal common good by ensuring that it is indeed used as a forum for authentic communication.

Epilogue

Beyond the "Local":

Ethics within a Community of Moral Discourse

I have demonstrated how one can do liberation-postcolonial ethics using discourse analysis that privileges those in the margins and/or vernacular categories. This method necessarily leads to a plurality of theologies and thus to the question of which of these theologies can be considered justifiable. Charles Curran emphasizes how the discernment of the ecclesial community plays a vital role in the validation of a theology.

As individuals in our pursuit of truth we are limited by our own finitude. We see only one part of the pie. The limited vision can bring about distortion in moral analysis and conclusions. . . . The Church as a community which exists over time and space helps to overcome the limitations which characterize every individual human being who exists in a particular culture, a particular place, and a particular time.[1]

---

[1] Charles E. Curran, "The Teaching Function of the Church in Morality," in *Moral Theology: Challenges for the Future: Essays in Honor of Richard A. McCormick, SJ*, ed. Charles E. Curran (New York: Paulist Press, 1990), 166.

In the Catholic Church, this mediation of Christian communities operates on the level of the conscientious faithful in general (as implied in the acceptance of theological terms such as *sensus fidelium*, public opinion, and public reception), theological communities, and the magisterium.[2]

The Christian communities as context of validation should not be construed, however, as a homogeneous collective that is free from the dynamics of power relations. What we have in these communities is a plurality of perspectives that may not necessarily agree in their reading of a cultural practice or tradition.

There is, however, an epistemological advantage in considering a multiplicity of perspectives in theological and scientific communities. When a group is homogeneous, it is possible that some background assumptions become invisible to them. The more points of view (that are not necessarily uniform) represented within a theological/scientific community, the more reflexive people become—and thus, the less prone scientific theories/theologies are to "idiosyncratic individual subjective preferences" or morally objectionable group biases.[3] This is why it is important that epistemic or knowing communities be composed of subjects from a variety of contextual-cultural perspectives.

To facilitate ideology criticism and discernment within Christian communities, I propose the following conditions for

---

[2] That this process should respect the principle of subsidiarity has been emphasized as well by Pope Francis, at least on the level of the teaching authority of bishops, in his apostolic exhortation *Evangelii Gaudium*: "It is not advisable for the pope to take the place of local bishops in the discernment of every issue which arises in their territory. In this sense, I am conscious of the need to promote a sound 'decentralization.'" Pope Francis, *Evangelii Gaudium*, no. 16 (2013), http://www.vatican.va/holy_father/francesco/apost_exhortations/documents/papa-francesco_esortazione-ap_20131124_evangelii-gaudium_en.html.

[3] Helen Longino, "Multiplying Subjects and the Diffusion of Power," *Journal of Philosophy* 88 (1991): 666–74.

effective community mediation.[4] First, there should exist recognized channels for criticism on the grassroots, pastoral, and professional levels (e.g., basic communities, pastoral sessions, journals, and colloquia). Second, the different theological/ecclesial communities should explicate the shared standards they are using so that those whose theological/ethical judgments are being criticized would know the criteria by which their judgments are being assessed. These criteria ideally comprise both the scientific norms and moral ideals of the community.[5] Third, it is necessary for the Christian communities to be responsive to the ongoing critical discussion. The aim

---

[4] I have appropriated these conditions from Helen Longino, philosopher of science. Helen Longino, "The Fate of Knowledge in Social Theories of Science," in *Socializing Epistemology*, ed. Frederick Schmitt (Lanham, MD: Rowman and Littlefield, 1994), 135–57.

[5] The following is an example of the hermeneutical principles (ethical criteria/norms) drawn up by the Asian EATWOT women which take into consideration differences of women based on class, race, religion, and ethnicity: "The Asian Women's hermeneutical principle interprets as in accordance with God's design: whatever promotes genuine dialogue among people of different cultures, religions and ideologies; whatever fosters equality, unity, justice and peace in all personal and social relationships; whatever empowers women and other marginalized people in our cultures and societies; whatever promotes communities of men and women characterized by sharing and mutuality, joy and freedom; whatever respects and protects creation." See EATWOT Women, *Patriarchy in Asia and Asian Women's Hermeneutical Principle* (Metro-Manila: EATWOT, 1991), 24. These ethical ideals are not extraneous to Scriptures, the *norma normans non normata*, but constitute rather the world in front of the Scripture text (Ricoeur's "world of the text"), i.e., the truth claims of the text for us today. The effective history of the Scripture generates a notion of discipleship today that is richer than what the original authors could have conceived. See Agnes Brazal, "Feminist Ideology Criticisms, the Bible, and the Community," *MST Review* 2, no. 2 (1999): 97–117; see also Reimund Bieringer, "The Normativity of the Future: The Authority of the Bible for Theology," in *Normativity of the Future: Reading Biblical and Other Authoritative Texts in an Eschatological Perspective*, ed. Reimund Bieringer and Mary Elsbernd (Leuven: Peeters, 2010), 27–45.

of dialogue here is not primarily to come up with a general and universal consensus on meaning but to allow for the refinement, correction, rejection, and ideological critique of interpretations. Fourth, there should be equality of intellectual authority within the Christian communities. This Habermasian criterion[6] holds that discourse and argumentation are distorted by dominating structures. The lack of women and members of other racial and minority groups within a theological community or magisterium, which consequently allows the white male paradigm to predominate, is a violation of the equality criterion.

To the above four conditions for effective ideology criticism, I add a fifth: requiring the granting of partial epistemological privilege (first hearing) to marginalized groups within the Christian communities.[7] Listening to the voice of the victims of society's theories and assertions is important epistemologically—as Edward Schillebeeckx points out—because experiences of suffering show a prereflective awareness of what should not be and an incipient realization of what things ought to be like.[8] Granting partial epistemological privilege means that theological communities should support the development of theories from the standpoint of the marginalized. This also

---

[6] For Jürgen Habermas, an ideal speech situation exists when there is freedom and equal access for all the participants in discourse to put forward their interpretations, justifications, objections or refutations. Otherwise, the result or the consensus would be less than rational, meaning that it is not the product of the force of the better argument but of hidden or open manipulations. Jürgen Habermas, "On Systematically Distorted Communication," *Inquiry* 13 (Autumn 1970): 205–18.

[7] On Longino's openness to the notion of partial epistemological privilege, see Helen Longino, *Essential Tensions—Phase Two: Feminist, Philosophical, and Social Studies of Science*, in *A Mind of One's Own: Feminist Essays on Reason and Objectivity*, ed. Louise Antony and Charlotte Witt (Boulder, CO: Westview Press, 1992), 270.

[8] Edward Schillebeeckx, OP, *God, the Future of Man* (New York: Sheed and Ward, 1968), 154–55.

requires that theologians reinvent themselves as other,[9] which means that they consider already the perspectives of the marginalized even from the beginning of the process of doing theology. The epistemological privilege granted to "others" is partial in the following senses. First, when a subordinated group has assumed a more dominant position, it no longer enjoys this privilege. Second, the interpretations from the perspective of marginalized groups still have to be subjected to critical analysis or to an evaluation vis-à-vis the publicly shared standards of the larger Christian community. These interpretations from the perspective of a particular oppressed group can either challenge, or still be challenged by, the standpoint especially of other marginalized groups within the Christian community.

These conditions imply the need for a church that can be a forum for the adjudication of competing claims. The representation of different voices in the church (conscientious faithful, theological communities, and magisterium) can guard against morally objectionable group biases to predominate and thus help in the discernment on the justifiability or not of a particular theological/ethical/pastoral assertion.

In doing liberation-postcolonial ethics, the employment of discourse analysis allows for the analysis of a plurality of perspectives on praxis/theory, which have to be discerned in the light of Scripture and tradition. In this hermeneutic mediation, the Christian communities' moral discourse plays a direct role in the validation of a theological/ethical/pastoral assertion. The representation of a plurality of perspectives in the faith communities, especially those of marginalized groups, heightens reflexivity and strengthens ideology criticism in the discourses of the local, regional, and global communities.

---

[9] Sandra Harding coined the phrase "reinventing ourselves as other" to refer to this way of seeking knowledge that takes into account the standpoint of "others." See Sandra Harding, *Whose Science? Whose Knowledge?: Thinking from Women's Lives* (Milton Keynes: Open University Press, 1991), 268–95.

Index